TEACHING THROUGH PLAY

TEACHING THROUGH PLAY
Teachers' thinking and classroom practice

Neville Bennett
Liz Wood
Sue Rogers

Open University Press
Buckingham • Philadelphia

Open University Press
Celtic Court
22 Ballmoor
Buckingham
MK18 1XW

email: enquiries@openup.co.uk
world wide web: www.openup.co.uk

and

325 Chestnut Street
Philadelphia, PA 19106, USA

First Published 1997
Reprinted 1998, 2001

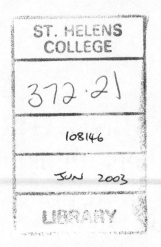

Copyright © Neville Bennett, Elizabeth Wood, Sue Rogers 1997

A catalogue record of this book is available from the British Library

ISBN 0 335 19732 9 (pb)   0 335 19733 7 (hb)

Library of Congress Cataloging-in-Publication Data
Bennett, Neville, 1937–
    Teaching through play : teachers thinking and classroom practice /
Neville Bennett, Elizabeth Wood, Sue Rogers.
        p.   cm.
    Includes bibliographical references and index.
    ISBN 0–335–19733–7 (hb). — ISBN 0–335–19732–9 (pb)
    1. Play. 2. Early childhood education—Activity programs.
I. Wood, Elizabeth, 1955– . II. Rogers, Sue, 1961– .
III. Title.
LB1139.35.P37B46   1996
372.21—dc20   96–19875
                                                          CIP

Typeset by Graphicraft Ltd, Hong Kong
Printed in Great Britain by Biddles Ltd, www.biddles.co.uk

CONTENTS

Acknowledgements   vi

1   Play: rhetoric and reality   1

2   Teacher thought and action: theory and method   18

3   Teachers' theories of play   31

4   Theory into practice   57

5   Changing theories and practice   79

6   Teaching through play: retrospect and prospect   116

Appendices
A   Teacher biographies   133
B   Interview schedule   135
C   Concept map of key ideas   138
D   Jennie's interpretations of learning through play   139

References   141
Index   147

ACKNOWLEDGEMENTS

We wish to record our gratitude first and foremost to the nine reception class teachers who cooperated so willingly and enthusiastically with us throughout the whole of the 1994/5 school year. Not only did they give us open access to their thoughts and practices in their classrooms, but they also devoted several Saturdays to our group meetings. The quality of our data is testimony to their efforts.

We also want to take this opportunity to thank in particular three people who operated behind the scenes, the quality of whose work substantially enhanced the analysis of our data. These were Sue Lumb, who so effectively and accurately transcribed all the interviews, Christobel Owens, whose meticulous analysis underpinned the shape of the initial concept map of teachers' theories (Appendix C: key ideas), and Nigel Weaver who so effectively produced it.

Last, but by no means least, our thanks are due to the Economic and Social Research Council, whose grant made this study possible.

CHAPTER 1

PLAY: RHETORIC AND REALITY

INTRODUCTION

Early childhood education is underpinned by a long-established tradition which emphasizes the central role of play in early learning and development. This is based predominantly on ideological, philosophical and educational principles derived from the work of Montessori, Isaacs and Steiner, amongst others (Bruce, 1987; Anning, 1991). The ideological base, described variously as the 'common law' or the 'nursery inheritance', has established a framework of general principles about childhood, children and how they should be educated, which have had an enduring influence on education in the early years.

The child-centred ideology which has emerged from this tradition incorporates several fundamental tenets regarding play. Children need to play and, in doing so, reveal their ongoing needs, which then shape the curriculum offered. This is tailored to individual interests which the teacher supports, maintaining respect for the children's intentions. A direct relationship between play and learning is assumed. Play is considered to be such an educationally powerful process that learning will occur spontaneously, even if an adult is not present. However, this central belief in the value of play to young children's learning is not borne out by empirical evidence and, in spite of continued endorsements, its place in the curriculum remains problematic. Why is this the case?

Ideologically the case for play may be strong but it is debatable whether this provides a coherent framework to guide practice. McAuley and Jackson (1992) maintain that this ideological inheritance has been informed by three distinct elements: received opinion, practical experience and prescriptive theory. It has not been underpinned by the findings of systematic research, or by critical analysis:

The 'common law' appears to have been compacted to a lowest common denominator, a baseline provision, which is, paradoxically, honoured again and again. This might in part owe something to a lack of critical training, compounded over the years by incoming influences that are improperly reviewed or simply stitched together and result in conceptual confusion.

(McAuley and Jackson, 1992: 30)

The origins of this conceptual confusion can be found in the ideological tradition, which is characterized by disparity rather than coherence.

TRADITIONS AND IDEOLOGIES

The work of the pioneer educators is examined by Bruce (1987) and Anning (1991). Their analyses reveal that although play has been elevated to *the* way of learning in early childhood, there are many disagreements among the pioneer educators. Each had distinct ideas about the role and value of play, which were related to concepts of freedom, innocence, naturalness and nurturing a child's full potential. They designed curricula which integrated their ideologies with their practice. For example, Froebel's philosophy supports an informally structured approach, whereas Montessori and Steiner suggest a greater degree of formality (Bruce, 1987). But by recommending different types of graded apparatus, resources and teaching methods to achieve their goals, all embody some degree of formality and structure.

Free play is regarded differently. Both Froebel and Montessori believed that children learn best from self-directed activity which is linked to intrinsic motivation. Montessori's provision of a child-sized environment was not designed to stimulate fantasy play, but to enable children to get closer to reality through a personal voyage of discovery. To this end she distrusted imagination, but utilized some but not all aspects of play to further children's social and cognitive development. In contrast, Froebel had an almost mystical belief in the value of spontaneous play (Anning, 1991) and invested it with symbolic significance. He emphasized the value of free play as an integrating mechanism which stimulates language and reveals the unity of feelings, thoughts and actions. By focusing on play, these and other educators in 19th-century Europe were striving to change the rather harsh attitudes towards children then current, and to introduce more enlightened approaches to their development, care and education. Similar trends were evident in Britain, influenced strongly in the 20th century by the empirical research of Susan Isaacs.

Isaacs argued that the significance of play lies in both the imaginative meaning and the cognitive value. From her observations of young children at the Malting House School, both imaginative and manipulative play were seen as the starting points which lead to the child's discovery, reasoning and thought. Play was conceptualized as a continuous moving back and forth between fantasy and reality in which children reveal their intellectual and emotional needs. This accords with the psychoanalytic tradition established by Sigmund Freud and Melanie Klein, in asserting that symbolic and fantasy play in particular have a cathartic function which enables children to work through deep emotional problems, inner conflicts and anxieties. Play has an educational and developmental function as it enables children to control their behaviour and accept the limitations of the real world, and furthers the development of the ego and a sense of reality.

Isaacs acknowledged that play is not the only means by which the child comes to discover the world, but saw it as 'supremely the activity which brings him psychic equilibrium in the early years' (1933: 425). In this respect, the role of the educator was mainly passive, providing an appropriate environment, but essentially leaving children to make their own choices and express their creative spirit. Isaacs's work continued the tension between allowing a high degree of freedom in play, with little adult intervention, and 'training' children in acceptable behaviour and social relationships. The latter demanded an active role for the educator as the child 'needs the help of external restraints in learning to deflect and control his own impulses, particularly the aggressive ones' (1933: 429).

The theoretical orientations to learning and development in Isaacs's work are behavioural, maturational and psychoanalytic. Each has contributed to the classic theories of play but, as Hughes (1991) points out, no single theory has ever been able completely to explain the significance of play in children's development, and the pedagogical implications have rarely been explored in any depth. Isaacs implicitly supports the romantic, child-centred ideology with its notions of freedom, children's rights and adults' responsibility to respect those. But it is difficult to defend this unequivocally both in theoretical and practical terms. On the one hand, the 'shaping and moulding' approach supports interventionism by the teacher. On the other, the 'unfolding and flowering' approach indicates a 'watching and waiting' role. Both have radically different implications for how the curriculum is conceptualized and enacted in practice, and for the role of play.

The apparent contradictions between these standpoints are explored by Bruce (1987). She attempts to reassess the ideological base and defines ten commonly agreed principles which are related to a modern context and are based on more recent theoretical trends. However, this synthesis is uncritical and is supported mainly by anecdotal evidence.

Furthermore, the ten principles are specified at a general level, and clear guidance on how these might translate into a coherent curriculum, and what the knowledge base is of that curriculum, is not given. Drummond (1989) argues that there is considerable consensus in the field, based on 'fine-sounding aims', which conceals a conceptual vacuum. As such, many early years practitioners have difficulty in justifying their aims, articulating their principles through their practice and, in particular, defining what constitutes an appropriate pedagogy. Without this underpinning, principles are likely to become little more than mantras which are recycled for familiarity in times of stress (Wood and Attfield, 1996). McAuley and Jackson (1992) also question the relevance of this ideological tradition because it emphasizes theories of child development rather than theories of learning. They challenge Bruce's 'consensus' and argue that the bewildering variety of ideas do not constitute a unified theory. Furthermore, 'allegiances to the common law have often lain behind resistance to change' (1992: 32). This allegiance is based largely on untested assumptions. In order to obtain a more critical view of the significance of play in early childhood, evidence from research needs to be examined.

PERSPECTIVES FROM RESEARCH ON PLAY

Because of the disparate nature of play, research has focused on different aspects in different contexts, and links between findings and classroom practice are not always made. It has also been bedevilled by the search for a definition of what play is and what it does for the child. Play is used as a broad term which covers a wide range of activities and behaviours which may serve a variety of purposes according to the age of the child. Pellegrini (1991) argues for a flexible approach to definitions which does not limit interpretations. He suggests that play can be defined according to three dimensions:

1 Play as disposition.
2 Play as context.
3 Play as observable behaviour.

(1991: 214)

Play as disposition includes intrinsic motivation, attention, exploration, nonliteral behaviours, flexibility and active engagement. The context of play is usually familiar and stress-free, and involves free choice. The criteria for play as observable behaviour are based on Piaget's three stages of play – functional, symbolic and games with rules – which evolve through early childhood. The more of these criteria that are met across the three dimensions, the more playful a child's behaviour. Thus children move along a continuum from pure play to non-play, a concept which avoids making a dichotomy between work and play and the value judgements that are implied in that. This is helpful for teachers, as they may have their own definitions of play, which relate to the contexts in which they work. Conceptualizing play and work as a continuum also acknowledges the fact that work-like, or at least non-playful, activities can also promote children's learning effectively, particularly if they incorporate some of the above dispositions such as intrinsic motivation, attention, and active engagement.

Bruce (1991) suggests that the word 'play' is too broad to be useful and that only 'free-flow' play truly encapsulates its essence. She states 12 distinguishing features of free-flow play which she sees as being concerned primarily with the ability and opportunity to wallow in ideas, experiences, feelings and relationships. Free-flow play is also distinguished by its irregular and chaotic nature, is difficult to predict and has no products or outcomes. Bruce draws on chaos theory in an attempt to explore the features of free-flow play but offers no empirical evidence to underline its benefits and does not demonstrate how chaos theory might usefully inform practice.

There is substantial evidence for the benefits of fantasy or sociodramatic play, perhaps because this tends to be a dominant form of play in early childhood and integrates a wide variety of behaviours. Smilansky (1990) argues that sociodramatic play either uses learning-relevant capacities or contributes to their development. These are defined as internal cognitive processes which are externalized through children's behaviour in their play and include imagination, creativity, symbolization, behaving in 'as if' and 'what if' mode to convey and sustain pretence, all of which contribute to social competence. Smilansky (1990) supports the concept of play tutoring – the direct intervention of an adult to encourage these skills and behaviours. Intervention increases the frequency, duration and complexity of the children's play, with increased levels of linguistic and cognitive competence. However, it has been questioned whether it is the play or the tutoring which led to these positive effects.

In contrast Meckley (1994a) found a sophisticated range of behaviours in the play of 4- and 5-year-old children without the presence of an adult. She studied children's play in a nursery classroom over a five-month period to understand its social organization. The children demonstrated competence in how they constructed play themes and events, revealing patterns of behaviour and communication which indicated shared and multiple meanings. The study shows that children have a repertoire of procedures and techniques for negotiating roles, plans, actions and objects in play. Far from being chaotic, their sociodramatic play reveals an inherent rule system which is often shared through metacommunication – verbal and non-verbal signals which convey meaning, intentions and the sequence of the play. It also reveals a consistent, ordered and interconnected structure which enables the players to share knowledge with or communicate meaning to other players (Meckley, 1994b).

This research has several implications. Sociodramatic play may be a more complex form of activity than has been previously recognized, and children need sustained bouts of play in order to develop expertise and confidence. The teacher should recognize that play can be a serious business which involves rehearsal, repetition and mastery. Increased levels of competence can enhance the quality and complexity of play which in turn make a substantial contribution to learning and development. In this sense, play does have products and outcomes though they may only be discernible through sustained observation. Thus children need to learn how to become good players to obtain the benefits of different activities.

There is some disagreement as to whether play provides contexts for learning new, or consolidating existing, behaviours, knowledge and skills. Fromberg's (1987) overview of research on play indicates that it serves a multiplicity of functions which depend crucially on interaction between adults and children. A consistent theme here is that children need to be taught how to play through modelling, as being a competent player does not always emerge spontaneously. Under such conditions, children then demonstrate improved verbal communication, social and interactional skills, creative use of play materials, problem-solving skills, imagination and divergent thinking skills. It is hypothesized that these positive outcomes have further benefits in later learning as children develop positive self-esteem and higher levels of cognitive competence.

Many of the studies cited by Fromberg are small-scale, experimental and psychological in orientation. She recommends that in order to be more relevant to practitioners, research needs to focus on both content and context in naturalistic settings so that better decisions about the curriculum can be made. For practitioners, a unified theory of play is difficult to find as the case for play is not so much weak as inconclusive. However, teachers wishing to justify play in the curriculum will find evidence from theory and research which underlines the value of play to early learning and development. In spite of the limitations of the ideological and theoretical base in early childhood education, there is continued support for play, but evidence suggests that this is not realized consistently in practice.

RESEARCH ON PLAY IN PRACTICE

Evidence from research on play in preschool and school settings indicates that the rhetoric of play is not realized in practice. Parry and

Archer (1975) argue that there are two levels of play: one merely keeps the children occupied, the other contributes to their educational development. In their view, play can sometimes look good with the children actively involved, and yet lack the elements which contribute towards educational growth. However, the lack of a precise method for distinguishing these two levels has hampered objective evaluation of play and its relationship to learning.

Sylva *et al.* (1980) evaluated play according to the degree of cognitive challenge. They studied children in preschool settings and distinguished between complex and simple play in order to ascertain the level of cognitive challenge in different activities. They assessed complexity by observing behavioural signs of inner cognitive processes and children's transformations of materials and people in their make-believe play. These definitions were supplemented by experienced practitioners' observations and classifications of complex and simple play. The study found that certain activities such as art, constructional activities and structured tasks were classified as 'high yield' as they offered cognitive challenge. These all provided a definite goal structure, with materials that provided 'real-world' feedback and goals that were usually chosen by the children. That is, they show the child whether a given sequence of behaviours has worked or not. Cognitive complexity, particularly for older children, was associated with adult interaction:

> This kind of enabling interaction is what many teachers and playgroup leaders aspire to and indeed does take place. Note, however, that it occurs mostly with older children and that, although extremely rich, each child experiences very little of it in a day.
>
> (1980: 75)

It was found that many adult interactions were focused on 'housekeeping' and managerial activities and consisted of 'domestic chat', which was unlikely to provide the substance of high cognitive challenge.

In contrast moderate yield activities included manipulative and small world toys. These often provided a 'cover' for observation, or just rest, and there was very little risk or fear of failure. Low complexity tasks rarely involved goals and seemed to be motivated by the desire for the pleasure of physical exercise or of repetition. Here there was little opportunity for planning, feedback or correction. This study relied predominantly on the researchers' interpretations of the data and did not include the aims, intentions and perspectives of the teachers or playgroup leaders. Hence their 'voice' was missing.

Similarly Meadows and Cashdan (1988) are critical of the scarcity and poor quality of adult–child interactions in nurseries:

> It seems to be the case that teachers who are operating a 'free play' regime do not interact with their children in stimulating ways, nor

do they have sustained conversations; they do their educational work indirectly through providing stimulating materials rather than teaching directly or playing themselves. In this they are true to the method of 'play way' – they are leaving the children free to stimulate themselves, to be creative and to learn at their own rate.

(1988: 33)

This play/work divide reflects the dilemmas surrounding the role of the teacher in play, and the primacy of child-initiated activity, and links directly to the ideological tradition and the constructivist principles of Piaget who advocated that children must actively construct knowledge for themselves. But does this level of independent learning actually happen in a free play regime? Meadows and Cashdan found that children were contented and busy, but three things were rare: sustained conversation or play with an adult, high complexity of play activities, and lively, purposeful involvement leading to creative, exciting discovery (1988: 39).

On the basis of this evidence they recommend that the traditional free play curriculum should be re-thought because the conditions for learning are not always present in the range of activities presented. In order for learning to be effective and efficient, children need to learn a range of sophisticated cognitive strategies. They recommend a social-constructivist model based on 'tutorial dialogue' which brings together children's and teachers' intentions in a reciprocal relationship. This enables teachers to scaffold children's learning and teach them how to become self-running problem-solvers.

Similar findings, again in preschool settings, are revealed by Hutt et al. (1989). Free choice of a range of play activities was the dominant form of organization in all the settings. Children's activity spans increased when an adult was present but periods of concentrated adult attention to an activity or an individual child were brief and were subject to constant interruptions arising from the fluidity of the free play situation. The adults' expectations for different activities were not always fulfilled. For example, dry sand was thought to assist imaginative play and develop children's social skills but in practice

the activities of the children in dry sand were highly stereotyped and repetitive, comprising largely of pouring sand from one container or another and the children had little or no interaction either with each other or with adults.

(Hutt et al., 1989: 212)

Similar observations were made of water play with the adult's role 'often merely monitorial, preventing or clearing up spills'. Fantasy play was held to be very important for preschool children but its supposed benefits again were not realized. The recommendations of this study were broad-ranging, including greater attention to aims and how they might be realized with more adult involvement, detailed planning, evaluation and record-keeping, clear aims and intentions, and an enabling structure.

The rhetoric surrounding play is not realized in preschool settings, in spite of their freedom to adopt a play-based curriculum with the benefit of generous staffing ratios. Promoting learning through play in reception classes is even more problematic given the different constraints and demands on teachers' time. In King's (1978) study, the rhetoric of the early childhood ideology apparently defined the teachers' roles and their practice. But in practice 'three R's' work dominated the curriculum, there was little free choice and the teachers rather than the children determined the pace of development. Play was seen as a prelude to work, particularly for younger or immature children. The teachers defined the learning content of play activities, but this was not always communicated to the children. Hence the children's perceptions of the purposes of play differed from those of the teachers. Play was considered to be the natural activity of children, but was constrained in the classroom by the availability of resources and the teachers' underlying intentions. Thus espoused notions of freedom, naturalness and childhood innocence were not given free rein.

Concerns about the quality of educational experiences offered to 4-year-old children in reception classes have been expressed consistently as the age at which children enter reception classes has gradually fallen to nearer 4 than 5 years old. Although a 'nursery style', play-based curriculum is advocated for this age group, and is supported by practitioners, there is little evidence of this in practice. In a study by Sestini (1987), play activities were provided but were implicitly devalued as teachers focused their attentions on other tasks – predominantly literacy and numeracy:

> most play activities in school served social functions and there was little evidence of cognitive challenge . . . Children's expectations of play in school were constrained, not only by limited resources, space and time, but also by their 'orientation' to play as a peer group social activity, not as an activity which promotes learning.
> (1987: 27)

Few of the play activities had the criteria for cognitive challenge defined in Sylva et al.'s study (1980). Sestini concludes that a redefining of the teacher's role is necessary for the potential of play to be realized:

> The teacher's role is demanding – provider of stimulating materials, observer, alert to children's interests and using knowledge of

how best to develop social and intellectual competencies in children who are at different levels and have different needs.

(1987: 30)

Similar conclusions are reached by Stevenson (1987) who found that reception teachers organize themselves to be involved in work while the children are involved in play. These themes recur in studies by Bennett and Kell (1989) and Cleave and Brown (1991) which examined the needs and quality of learning experiences of 4-year-olds in school. Again the importance of play is expressed by the teachers, with reference to the early childhood ideology, and they are clear about the potential purposes and benefits of play. However, Bennett and Kell observed play to be 'very limited and very limiting':

> The teachers appear to have low expectations of it, often acting as a time filler, and far too frequently there was no clear purpose or challenge, a lack of pupil involvement, very little monitoring or attempt at extension. In other words, play activities tended not to provide learning experiences of an acceptable quality.

(1989: 79)

Cleave and Brown (1991) note that some teachers tried to avoid the play/work distinction by labelling everything as work, but the children persisted in this distinction. Choosing continued to be equated with play, whilst teacher-directed activity was equated with work. In the best examples of more appropriate practice, teachers made deliberate attempts to accord all types of activity equal status, primarily through their involvement. Again observations revealed that this intention was not always borne out in practice.

Further evidence of the problems faced by reception class teachers is provided by Ofsted (1993). In a quarter of the classes inspected there was sometimes an over-emphasis on sedentary tasks and, where this occurred, insufficient time was left for practical activity or exploratory play. However, the quality of learning through play presented a dismal picture in more than a third of schools' where it was used predominantly as recreational rather than educational. The distinction between poor and effective practice is specified:

> In the poorer classes teachers over-directed work and under-directed play. They used play as a reward for finishing work or as an occupational or holding device. By contrast, in the effective classes, play was used positively to develop children's abilities across a wide range of activities.

(1993: 10)

Striking the right balance in the curriculum is a difficult task. Nevertheless, the gap between rhetoric and reality is difficult to account for.

Play is widely regarded as providing rich contexts for children's learning but this is not always evident in practice. The rhetoric of play is underpinned more by assumptions than by consistent evidence, and it appears the play in school and preschool settings presents some difficult problems for practitioners. Atkin (1991) suggests that there is a general mistrust of play, which is based on bipolar constructs. Thus if children are playing, they are not working. Play is for leisure and fun, whilst work is the serious business of life (Anning, 1991). Play is often regarded as a process which promotes learning (Moyles, 1989), but may not necessarily result in any tangible outcomes. In the current educational climate this makes play susceptible to criticism, as teachers have to provide evidence of learning and attainment which can be recorded and reported to parents and other professionals. Play is notoriously difficult to evaluate, particularly free-flow play, which tends to be spontaneous and unpredictable. There is an emphasis on learning through socialization with other children, rather than from adults. This militates against the sort of involvement which would enable skilled educators to enhance learning and, at the same time, make informed assessments to feed into the cycle of curriculum planning.

Guha (1988) argues that a distinction should be made between play 'as such', and play 'in schools', as the kind of play which has to be justified in schools is the meeting place where children and teachers share intentions. The evidence suggests that there are three main areas which need to be addressed to reconcile the rhetoric–reality divide: theoretical perspectives on teaching and learning, the role of the teacher and the nature of the curriculum offered.

CURRENT PERSPECTIVES ON LEARNING

Even where play is considered to further learning and development, the relationship to pedagogy is not straightforward. Thus different theories of play have different implications for classroom practice. Piaget's theories of learning have had a dominant influence on classroom practice. He argues that play can facilitate learning by encouraging children to assimilate new material into existing cognitive structures (1962). It is essentially a consolidating activity which promotes practice, rehearsal and repetition, allowing children then to move on to new learning through the process of accommodation which involves changing or extending cognitive structures. Piaget's constructivist theories are characterized by active learning, first-hand experience and intrinsic motivation as the spurs to cognitive development, all of which are usually evident in children's play. His argument that development leads learning through clearly defined ages and stages has been interpreted to imply a reactive role for the teacher – the 'watching and waiting' approach. Play has a revelatory function which indicates children's developing needs and interests which they should be allowed to pursue. The role of the teacher is to respond to their self-initiated activity, but to allow children actively to construct knowledge for themselves. In practice, this theoretical standpoint has led to curricula based on a substantial degree of self-choice which fitted well with the liberal, child-centred ideology derived from the work of the earlier pioneer educators.

In contrast, the social-constructivist theories of Lev Vygotsky and Jerome Bruner emphasize interaction with a 'more knowledgeable other' as a significant part of the learning process. Vygotsky (1978) regarded play as a leading source of development in the preschool years, but not the dominant form of activity. He argued that social interaction with peers and adults helps children to make sense and create meaning from experience within a shared cultural framework. It is specifically the means used within social interaction, particularly language, which lead learning and development. In the process, children acquire knowledge, information and tools for thinking and learning. Vygotsky (1978) proposed that learning occurs within a zone of proximal development. This represents the difference between the actual and potential developmental levels – what a child can do without assistance, and what he or she can learn to do with the assistance of a more knowledgeable other, who may be an adult or a child. Play creates zones for proximal development because children are motivated to learn and can be enabled to move ahead of their current level of development, particularly if supported by a more skilled or knowledgeable other. Social interaction, imagination and symbolic transformations in play are seen as complex cognitive processes which, Vygotsky argued, can lead to higher forms of cognition (Newman and Holzman, 1993).

Similarly Bruner (1991) argues that play serves as a vehicle for socialization including teaching children about the nature of society's rules and conventions. They learn about roles, rules, relationships, friendship skills, appropriate forms of behaviour and about the consequences of their actions for other people. Play contexts create opportunities for children to set their own rules for acting out roles and themes and for determining the success of the play. The interactions between adults and children create a 'scaffold' for mediating learning. This reflects the notion that learning is both recursive and incremental and can be assisted by more knowledgeable others who actively model learning skills and processes, and transmit relevant knowledge. Social-constructivist theories are based on a complex model of teaching and learning which values both child-initiated and teacher-directed activities. These theories imply a proactive role for the teacher in creating challenging learning environments and providing appropriate assistance at the right time even in play activities.

THE ROLE OF THE ADULT

Lally (1989) notes that there is a natural tendency for adults to consider the activities they select for children as having the highest value, in spite of their apparent commitment to play. Yet observations of children's self-directed activities often reveal 'powerful evidence of children effectively directing their own learning, particularly if supported in the process by an adult' (1989: 9). This reflects a dilemma in trying to achieve a balance between children's rights to choose and be in control of their own learning and the teacher's responsibility to ensure that all children experience breadth, balance and progression. HMI considered that where children are left too much to themselves

> children's educational play may quickly degenerate into undemanding time-filling activities where the teacher's energies are spent coping more with the provision and organization of materials than with teaching the children.
>
> (DES, 1989: 33)

In contrast, Hall (1994) warns emotively against turning play from a joyful children-initiated experience into a mournful teacher-led experience. Such dichotomous perspectives on the teacher's role in play derive from the ideological tradition. In a child-centred ideology, Meadows and Cashdan characterize the role of the teacher as

> guide, friend, counsellor and facilitator. Teacher intervention should be of the gentlest kind, the teacher's main skill lying in the provision of appropriate materials for learning, and the structuring of the classroom context, both social and intellectual, so as to make learning more likely and attractive.
>
> (1988: 3)

There is an assumption that when children make their own choices, learning becomes a much more powerful activity. But in reality this is dependent on the range of choices available, the amount of interaction with more knowledgeable others (including peers and adults), the provision of supportive resources and the potential for activity to be connected to worthwhile learning. The reactive role contrasts with Smilansky's (1990) view that children's cognitive competence can be enhanced through play tutoring. Similarly, Shefatya (1990) argues that adult involvement in play increases children's fantasy play, and improves their cognitive, language and social development. However, the critical issue here is that the kinds of interactions used by the adults must be both supportive of and responsive to the child's needs and potential:

> Intervention should be skill oriented and not content oriented; that is the purpose is to provide children with tools to express and

actualize their needs, to experience roles that fascinate them to the fullest, and, accordingly, to enact and develop themes with content that interests them. It seems that the basic skills that should be emphasized at early age levels are the ones that characterize well-developed play of older children: role declaration; make believe with objects, actions and situations; co-operation; and elaboration of themes according to role. All of these should be supported with sensitivity to the child's level of play development and in congruence with the content the child is trying to express.

(Shefatya, 1990: 153)

These perspectives challenge two important assumptions about play. First, that children know spontaneously how to engage in different kinds of play. Second, that teachers and other adults have only a limited role as enablers and facilitators. Both Smilansky and Shefatya indicate that children sometimes need to learn how to play, and that teachers can actively assist in this process, thus supporting social-constructivist theories. Furthermore, children thus become increasingly skilled players and learners. This questions whether the *laissez-faire* approach advocated in child-centred ideology (King, 1978) gives teachers an integral role in the whole teaching–learning process and enables them to operate at the highest level of their skill. For example, teachers may claim that children spontaneously gain mathematical knowledge through a variety of experiences such as sorting and matching games, role play, constructional materials. However, as we have seen there is often a mismatch between assumptions and outcomes, particularly where the children's learning is not supported by the appropriate language to assist concept formation and cognitive processes.

Social-constructivist theories shift the emphasis towards an interactionist role in which the teacher is actively involved in children's play in ways that are sensitive to their meanings and intentions, but nevertheless move them forward in their learning. Wood and Attfield (1996) argue that in order for play to become more securely located within the curriculum framework, early childhood practitioners need to reclaim their pedagogical expertise and to state the complexity of an interactionist role which connects children with tools for thinking, learning and playing. Reciprocity between teachers and learners is the common ground for negotiating meaning and mediating cognitive development.

This implies that if we are to address critically the nature of children's learning through play, then we must also address the nature of teaching though play. The ideological tradition supports an emphasis on learning by discovery through self-initiated activities. This assumes a direct link between learning and playing, whatever the conditions, in which children teach themselves important cognitive skills. However, current theoretical perspectives dispute the primacy of discovery methods for young, inexperienced learners (Meadows, 1993). Seifert (1993) criticizes the predominantly passive role of early childhood educators in play. The 'watching and waiting' ideology does not reflect social-constructivist theories which view the role of the teacher as instrumental in helping children to acquire and organize knowledge and to make connections between areas of learning and experience. Seifert argues that in view of these theories, 'early childhood educators may need to re-think their frequent, pervasive commitment to curricular self-choice' (1993: 12). This is a clear challenge to what Seifert sees as predominantly *laissez-faire* approaches. However, as we have seen, this degree of interventionism in children's play is anathema to teachers for ideological reasons. For reception class teachers there may also be valid practical constraints on their time.

Johnson (1990) argues that play enables children to construct meaning from experience and can further cognitive development. Therefore teachers are in a unique position to support these processes and to help children realize the educational potential of play. If play provides a rich context for learning, then surely it must provide a rich context for teaching. Indeed, in examining the rhetoric–reality divide, teaching through play can be seen as the missing half of the equation. For many early childhood practitioners this will seem a challenging concept. However, recent trends in curriculum development for children under 5 indicate a change of focus.

CURRENT PERSPECTIVES ON THE EARLY CHILDHOOD CURRICULUM

In spite of the reservations outlined above, the need for a play-based curriculum for children under 5 continues to receive widespread support (Moyles, 1989, 1994; Bruce, 1991). In a report on the education of children under 5 (DES, 1989), HMI outline the importance of designing a broad and balanced curriculum in which play features strongly. There is a rejection of a *laissez-faire* approach here, as play is not seen as a free and wholly unstructured activity. There is a distinct emphasis on planned, purposeful play alongside the recognition that there are many other equally valuable ways of learning, some of which may be teacher-initiated. The curriculum focuses on children's cognitive, physical, social and emotional development but with clearer specification of the content of the curriculum in terms of knowledge, skills, values and attitudes. This is at variance with the broad developmental trends represented in the ideological tradition and recognizes forms of knowledge not as a contaminant of early childhood but as the essential building blocks of learning and development. The role of teachers and other educators is seen as essentially proactive in creating high quality learning environments and designing worthwhile activities.

This approach is also supported by the Rumbold Report (DES, 1990) which investigated the quality of educational experiences for children under 5:

> For young children, purposeful play is an essential and rich part of the learning process. Play is a powerful motivator, encouraging children to be creative and to develop their ideas, understanding and language. Through play, children explore, apply and test out what they know and can do.
>
> (DES, 1990: 7)

Both these reports establish frameworks within which an appropriate curriculum can be developed. They acknowledge that a high quality preschool curriculum is characterized by a range of factors, including clearly defined aims and objectives, differentiation for children with special educational needs, skilled interactions with adults, good home–school relationships, and the promotion of equal opportunities. These are seen as contributing to the development of children's self-awareness, self-confidence and success as learners. The need for flexibility in curriculum design is considered desirable because of the diversity of settings for children under 5. Both reports advocate the use of HMI's nine areas of learning and experience as an appropriate framework for planning and evaluating the curriculum, with purposeful play an integral part of this framework. The Rumbold Report states that in order for the potential value of play to be realized a number of conditions need to be fulfilled:

- sensitive, knowledgeable and informed adult involvement and intervention;
- careful planning and organization of play settings in order to provide for and extend learning;
- enough time for children to develop their play;
- careful observation of children's activities to facilitate assessment and planning for progression and continuity.

(DES, 1990: 11)

This framework provides a significant challenge to the rather loose structures which tend to characterize preschool settings and *laissez-faire* approaches to play. These enabling conditions also call into question some of the implicit assumptions of the ideological traditional underpinning play, particularly relating to adult involvement, and represent a significant shift towards social-constructivist theories. The potential value of play is acknowledged but the notion of purposeful play and worthwhile activities introduces some value judgements about what is considered to be educationally relevant for this age group. The notion of a play-based curriculum is also questioned, as the focus has gradually shifted towards the content and outcomes of children's learning rather than just the nature of the activities and experiences. Increasingly, early childhood educators have been encouraged to define both learning intentions and outcomes in relation to subject matter knowledge, and to ensure that the intellectual demands on children are matched to their developing skills and competences (Hall and Abbott, 1991; Moyles, 1994).

SUMMARY

The rhetoric of play does not appear to be realized in practice. Evidence suggests that there are significant problems relating to the nature and purposes of play in educational settings. Relying on a disparate ideological underpinning to justify play is insufficient since this has failed to provide a unified theoretical and pedagogical knowledge base to guide practice. There is little clarification of the nature of teaching and learning in play, the influence of different play contexts and the relationship of play to the curriculum. Reception children sit uncomfortably between preschool and Key Stage 1, so that a 'nursery style' curriculum for this age group is difficult to implement because of the different contexts and constraints which operate. Therefore they may experience an inappropriate curriculum with activities which are poorly matched to their characteristics as learners. If play is to be used in pursuit of more clearly defined educational purposes in line with contemporary recommendations, the quality of play in educational settings needs to be improved.

However, it is clear that if play is to be used for more clearly defined educational purposes, and to have a more secure place in the curriculum, then relying on the ideological tradition is insufficient. Suggestions for the improvement of practice are unlikely to emanate from this tradition, and its relevance to contemporary educational contexts has been questioned. In our view, an alternative way forward is by providing enhanced understandings of what actually happens in classrooms by exploring the relationship between teachers' theories of play and their practice. This is seen as the first necessary step in improving the quality of play.

CHAPTER 2

TEACHER THOUGHT AND ACTION: THEORY AND METHOD

INTRODUCTION

The consistent picture of play in early years classrooms being limited in frequency, duration and quality inevitably raises questions about the pedagogical processes, and the thinking and planning behind them, which serve to sustain such outcomes. For example, what theoretical, substantive and practical knowledge of play do teachers draw on in their planning? How do they transform this knowledge into worthwhile tasks and activities? What constraints in the classroom or school mediate the successful implementation or use of these activities? In other words, questions need to be asked about teachers' knowledge and beliefs that underpin their classroom practice.

Studies of teachers' knowledge, beliefs and theories are relatively recent. Clark and Peterson (1986) characterize research on teachers' theories as the smallest and youngest part of the literature on teacher thinking. Its purpose is, they argue, to make explicit the often implicit frames of reference through which teachers perceive and process information, on the assumption that a teacher's cognitive and pedagogical behaviours are guided by, and make sense in relation to, a personally held system of beliefs, values and principles.

Unfortunately the research effort since that time has been fragmented, and bedevilled by differences in assumptions and by technological confusion. Some hint of this can be gained from the terms used, and assumptions made, in the previous paragraph. Terms such as knowledge, beliefs, theories, thinking, values, principles and frames of reference are all used to characterize aspects of teachers' thinking. Clark and Peterson also make the assumption that this thinking guides teachers' classroom behaviour. In other words, the influence is clearly directional – thinking precedes, and leads to, action.

Indicative of the terminological problem is the list which Pope (1993) presents, which contains 23 terms used in studies of teacher thinking. Clandinin and Connelly (1987) and Fenstermacher (1994) similarly comment on the bewildering array of terms, and come to similar conclusions. The former conclude that 'People using different terms often appear in fact to mean much the same thing' (1987: 498), and the latter, after identifying a host of different types of teacher knowledge, including strategic, propositional, relational, craft, local, case, situated, tacit and personal, argued that 'These names do not necessarily refer to different types of knowledge' (1994: 6). Marland (1987: 504) condemns this state of affairs, arguing that the 'terminological babel in research on teacher thinking is causing confusion and impeding productive dialogue'.

Also reflective of this muddle are arguments about the distinction between knowledge and beliefs. Alexander and Dochy (1995) contend that explicit definitions or explanations of these terms are rarely offered, and conclude that it is unclear where the boundaries of these two fundamental concepts lie. Pajares (1992) also accepts that confusion exists around this distinction, and that there appears to be no consensus. Some continue to define knowledge and belief separately (Pajares, 1992; Nespor, 1987), and argue about their relative influence on action; however there is a growing tendency to regard them as synonymous, or envelop beliefs within definitions of knowledge. Kagan (1990), for example, states that she uses belief and knowledge interchangeably, and Alexander et al. (1991) similarly subsume beliefs within knowledge, by arguing that knowledge encompasses all a person knows or believes to be true, whether or not it is verified as true in some sort of objective or external way. Their definition of knowledge thus refers to an individual's personal stock of information, skills, experiences, beliefs and memories. This same definition is adopted for the study reported here.

Studies of teacher thinking have also been undertaken for different purposes. Bennett et al. (1996) identify six different purposes of research on teacher thinking, only one of which is pertinent here: i.e. those studies which have investigated the relationships between teachers' knowledge and aspects of classroom practice. This is a disparate group of studies in terms of terminology and methodological approach, but it shares the assumption that teachers' knowledge precedes, and/or guides, classroom practice. A selection of these studies is considered below.

Grossman et al. (1989) report relationships between the beliefs and practice of student teachers. They argue that although the nature and influence of teachers' beliefs about teaching, about students, about schools, and about subject matter on their practice is relatively unexplored territory in research on teaching what research has been carried out indicates that teachers' beliefs about teaching and learning are related to how they think about teaching, how they learn from their experiences, and how they conduct themselves in classrooms. In their own work with student teachers they found that their beliefs about the content that they teach influences both what they choose to teach, and how they choose to teach. Grossman *et al.* also found that teachers had different orientations to subject matter which influenced their choice of content to teach. They concluded that, among secondary student teachers at least, beliefs about subject matter were as powerful and influential as their beliefs about teaching and learning, a conclusion recently reiterated by Holt-Reynolds (1992).

Similar findings are reported at primary and secondary school level. Nespor (1987) found that the values placed on course content by secondary school teachers often influenced how it was taught, and claimed that teachers' belief systems are very important determinants of how teachers organize their world into task environments and define tasks and problems. He concluded that 'to understand teaching from teachers' perspectives we have to understand the beliefs with which they define their work' (1987: 323). Thompson (1992) overviewed research linking beliefs and practice in mathematics teaching in both primary and secondary schools. These indicate a high relationship between teachers' beliefs about mathematics and their actual practice, but a less consistent one between their general beliefs about teaching and their practice.

At primary level Richardson and her colleagues (1991) investigated the relationship between teachers' beliefs about the teaching of reading comprehension and their classroom practices in grades 4–6 (10–12-year-olds). They found that most categories of reading practices could be predicted accurately from teachers' beliefs. They concluded that genuine changes will come about only when teachers think differently about what is going on in their classrooms, and are provided with the practices to match their different ways of thinking.

Of particular interest to the study reported here are those investigations which have been undertaken into, or with, early years teachers. King (1978) analysed the beliefs, values and customs of infant teachers and suggested that they manifested a child-centred set of theories, or ideology – an ideology that related to such elements as developmentalism, individualism, play as learning, and childhood innocence. These elements were instrumental in helping teachers construct their conceptions of appropriate learning environments. The beliefs of these teachers about children and the learning process were, he argued, integral to what happened in the classroom.

Spodek, in researching the implicit theories of early years teachers, assumed a causal relationship between beliefs and practice: 'teachers' actions and classroom decisions are driven by their perceptions and beliefs' (1988: 13). He thus argued that in order to understand the nature of teaching, one must not only understand the behaviour of the teachers observed, but also the teachers' thought processes regarding teaching and the implicit theoretical systems that drive their processes. His study aimed to ascertain if there was a set of implicit theories that were held more generally by early childhood teachers. However, the findings are not easy to interpret since his theories seem to be synonymous with individual instances of beliefs and/or knowledge. Thus the number of 'implicit theories' held by teachers varied from 127 to 259. He concluded that teacher decisions in the classroom are opportunistic and rooted in personal practical knowledge rather than 'technical' knowledge of child development and learning theory.

Finally, Anning (1988) in a small-scale study of six teachers reported that the principles encapsulated in each of these teachers' beliefs about children's learning were clearly linked to the teaching strategies they identified. She thus concluded that teachers' theories are embedded in their practice.

The foregoing studies, although relatively scarce and involving small samples, eclectic methodological approaches and differing terminology, consistently report that teacher knowledge and beliefs are related to, predict, determine or indeed drive classroom practice. They also support the contention that knowledge and beliefs are often implicit, echoing Schoenfield's argument that 'belief systems shape cognition, even when one is not consciously aware of holding those beliefs' (1985: 35).

Nevertheless, this body of research provides only a limited understanding of the links between knowledge and practice, in part because few studies have incorporated contemporary thinking about the situated nature of teacher knowledge, or the potentially powerful effects of constraints in mediating teacher knowledge and action. Leinhardt (1988), for example, states that much of the knowledge teachers have about teaching is situated within the context of teaching. Situated knowledge of teaching has developed in a specific context and, within that context, is extremely powerful since it connects teaching events with particular environmental features such as classrooms, time of year, individual people, physical surroundings, specific pages of text, and more abstracted subject matter knowledge (cf. Brown and McIntyre, 1993).

Situated knowledge stresses 'know how', or what works and does not work in specific education contexts. These contexts are an important element in teacher learning, but they are also an important mediator between teachers' knowledge and practice. Clark and Peterson (1986) argue that the relationship between what we say and do is mediated by contextual constraints. As such a complete understanding of the process of teaching is not possible without an understanding of the constraints and opportunities that impinge on the teaching process. There is little empirical evidence on the nature and extent of these constraints, but Grossman and Stodolsky (1994) recently specified these for teaching in secondary schools:

> The work of teaching depends greatly on the specific grade level; the particular subject matter; the school's organisation, mission, culture and location and the district, state and national contexts in which teaching and learning occur. These multiple contexts affect teachers and students in myriad ways . . . contexts matter.
>
> (1994: 180)

In short, contexts can act, in their various ways, either to enable or to constrain the enactment of teacher theories in practice.

In summary, it is apparent that the research effort has been limited and diverse. Studies have been underpinned by different theoretical approaches embodying different assumptions about the relationship between thought and action. The central variables have been labelled differently, even if defined similarly, and these definitions have often disregarded, or confused, any distinction between knowledge and belief. It therefore remains unclear how thinking influences practice, and what factors mediate this influence. And in the early years field in particular there is a dearth of evidence on what aspects of teacher thinking influence what aspects of their pedagogy. Thus, in the specific, but crucial, area of play, there is no evidence of how teachers' understandings, values and beliefs about play inform their curriculum planning, selection of activities, teaching approaches or assessments of outcomes. Nor are there any indications of how the contexts in which teachers work constrain or enable the planning and enactment of play activities. It was the need for answers to these questions that motivated this piece of research, answers which, we believe, are necessary precursors to considerations of how to improve practice.

A MODEL OF TEACHER THOUGHT AND ACTION

A conceptual model of teacher thinking and classroom practice was needed to guide decisions on methodology and data collection. This was developed from an integration of the foregoing research literature with that in the wider field of classroom processes (see Alexander *et al.*, 1992; Bennett, 1992). This is shown in Figure 2.1.

Figure 2.1 draws on our definition of teacher knowledge as the teacher's personal stock of information, skills, experiences, beliefs and memories, and the assumption that sets of knowledge of different aspects of their work combine to become a theory or ideology. These theories can be narrow or broad. For example, a teacher's theory of play will draw on,

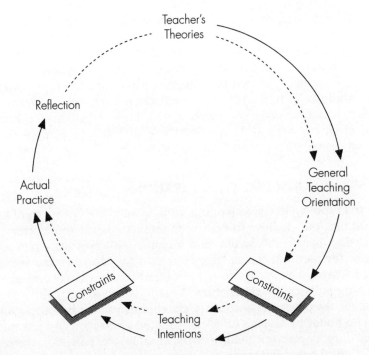

Figure 2.1   Hypothesized relationship of theory and action

and be built upon, a particular set of understandings and beliefs, but this theory of play will, in turn, be but one element of his or her broader theory of teaching in the early years, as King (1978) showed. He also contended that these theories were instrumental in the teacher's conceptions and constructions of appropriate learning environments. This is shown in the model as 'general teaching orientation' which incorporates teachers' pedagogical priorities, such as the provision of contexts for learning through play.

The extent to which teachers are able to fulfil their ideal teaching orientations through the activities that they plan for their children will depend on sets of mediating factors or constraints. The constraints which operate between teaching orientation and teachers' task intentions could include factors at classroom, school, local or national level, e.g. classroom space, the availability of resources and equipment, the number and characteristics of the children, school policy on class size and teaching assistance, perceptions of parental priorities, and the demands of the National Curriculum. Similarly, whether or not teachers' intentions are realized in practice will rest on another, but overlapping, set of constraints including the reaction of children to the activity, the amount of adult help, and the time, space and resources available.

Finally, whether, or how, practice changes, and the effect of those changes on teachers' theories, will depend on the extent to which teachers are able, enabled or willing to reflect on links between intentions and practice, and from these to their underpinning theories. This aspect is identified in the model by dotted lines because it was not our stated purpose in this study to examine the role of reflection in changes in practice or theories; it did nevertheless occur, as will be seen in Chapter 4, as an unintended, but very welcome, outcome of teachers' participation in the study.

METHODOLOGICAL CONSIDERATIONS

A central problem in research of this kind, as Feiman-Nemser and Floden (1986) point out, is how to get inside teachers' heads to describe their knowledge, beliefs and values, and Kagan (1990) presents a critique of many of the methods which have been used for accessing and assessing these. Most studies to date have been interpretive, i.e. concerned with describing individuals' experiences of reality, aiming for highly detailed studies for the purposes of understanding human action in context, influenced no doubt by Clark's (1986) oft-quoted phrase 'quality portraiture may be of more practical and inspirational value than reductionist analysis and technical prescriptiveness'.

Within this tradition, stories, narratives and portrayals have become important instruments of data collection. Narrative accounts of teaching aim to describe teaching in teachers' own words and to represent its real life complexity (Calderhead, 1996). The main claim for the use of narrative is that humans are story-telling organisms who, individually and socially, lead storied lives. The study of narrative is thus the study of the ways humans experience the world (Connelly and Clandinin, 1990; Gudmundsdottir, 1991). This claim is supported by psychologists like Bruner (1985, 1986), who has identified story-telling as one of two fundamentally different modes of human thought, standing in contrast to the analytic, linear way of thinking prevalent in logic, mathematics and the sciences. These, he claimed, constitute two different ways of knowing – one seeks formal means to verify truth, that is, explications that are context-free and universal, and the other establishes only verisimilitude – explications that are context-sensitive and particular. On these bases, Berliner (1992) too argues that the mind has a preference for stories: 'knowledge is contextualised, it is situated, it is enmeshed in webs of meaning'.

The utilization of story is often associated with the wider political issue of teacher empowerment, expressing an implicit critique of earlier studies of teaching which, it is claimed, tended to reduce the complexity of teachers' work and to privilege theoretical formulations over concerns of teachers themselves (Elbaz, 1990). For Elbaz stories most adequately constitute and present teachers' knowledge. However researchers have used stories in different ways. Some use them primarily as a methodological device – an effective way of presenting data which is rich and illuminating and which would otherwise be difficult to convey. For others it is methodology itself – the work consists of getting the narrative and using it to make a point about the work of teachers. And for some it is the very purpose of their work (Connelly and Clandinin, 1990; Elbaz, 1990).

However, running alongside the proliferation of narrative studies have been constant expressions of concern about the validity and meaning of the stories collected. The criticisms have focused on three areas – validity, generalizability and epistemic merit. Leinhardt (1990), from the perspective of gaining understandings of teachers' craft knowledge, contends that it is hard to know whether the teacher has concocted some magical brew to describe what he or she is doing, or whether the teacher is reporting the critical pieces of performance and knowledge. She urges that not all knowledge from teachers be considered wisdom. However, this is not an issue unique to teachers' stories. Bruner (1987) argues that autobiographical accounts in general are notably unstable, and that a rousing tale of life is not necessarily a 'right' account. Phillips (1993: 21), in decrying the lack of epistemological considerations in accounts of stories and narratives, makes a similar point: 'the fact that a story is credible tells us nothing – absolutely nothing – about whether it is true or false'. Carter, an advocate of narrative inquiry, thus warned that 'we cannot escape the basic problems of knowledge in our field by elevating teachers' stories to a privileged status' (1993: 9). She also warned of the difficulties of generalization. 'Generalizations from a story are at best precarious' (1993: 10).

Fenstermacher (1994) argues that teacher knowledge must meet evidentiary standards if it is to have epistemic merit, and criticizes narrative researchers for having scant regard for this. He states that there are a number of ways of warranting a knowledge claim – through evidence, or through the presentation of good reasons through reflection on the relationship between means and ends. This he calls practical reasoning, which he defines as a means for transforming the tacit quality of the teacher's knowing to a level of awareness that opens the possibility for reflective consideration. This, he argues, is the minimal form of warrant for practical action. In summary, therefore, the utilization of story as a valid method for the explication of teacher thinking and knowing is only acceptable to the extent that the knowledge acquired is, in some way, warranted.

Knowledge claims about action are equally problematic. Teachers' stories about classroom action have typically been acquired via stimulated recall techniques. Studies of teachers' interactive decision-making extensively used this technique, but doubts have been expressed about the validity of this procedure for that purpose (Yinger, 1986; Calderhead, 1987). However these doubts are restricted to research on interactive thinking. As Yinger concludes, 'stimulated recall is not a means of eliciting interactive thought or reflection-in-action, but rather a means to elicit reflection-on-action.' Used in this way it provides access to the ways in which teachers make sense of teaching episodes, and can elicit teachers' implicit theories and beliefs, as well as their understandings of the specific patterns of behaviour or interaction (Nespor, 1985).

However, here too there needs to be a requirement for teachers' reasons, explanations and justifications of their practice to provide the knowledge warrant. In fact, Fenstermacher argues that, if the researcher probes in a manner indicative of trust and mutual regard the teachers' reasons for acting as they did, the knowledge that was previously tacit may reach a conscious level of awareness. Once aware of it, the teacher can deliberate or reflect on it. As such this becomes a powerful means of teacher learning and, indeed, professional development (cf. Freeman, 1991).

RESEARCH DESIGN

The main aims of the study were threefold:

- to provide a clear specification of teachers' theories of play
- to ascertain the relationship between teachers' theories and their classroom practices
- to examine the perceived impact of mediating factors or constraints on this relationship.

These aims, and the associated research questions, required an interpretive approach. Erickson opted for the term interpretive to indicate an interest in 'Human meaning in social life and in its elucidation and exposition' (1986: 119). Or, as Walsh et al. more eloquently put it, 'At the heart of interpretive inquiry is a passion to understand the meaning that people are constructing in their everyday situated actions' (1993: 465). An interpretive stance automatically connotes a cooperative approach since understandings of participants' perspectives is not possible without extended interaction, which in turn requires a common agenda, and a sympathetic and empathic relationship between researcher and researched. In other words – research with, rather than research on, teachers.

The design was conceived in three cumulative stages, that is, each stage would build on analyses of the former, to create multiple layers of

Table 2.1 Research design

Stage 1	Narrative accounts by teachers focusing on how they integrate play into the curriculum
Teacher group	Discussion of initial map of key concepts and theories
Stage 2	Interviews with teachers based on the key themes derived from the analysis of the narratives
Teacher group	Validation of concept map of key themes Exploration of definitions and assumptions about play
Stage 3	Stimulated reflection-on-action through videotapes of teacher-selected episodes of play, post-video interviews and protocols of teacher intentions
Teacher group	Sharing reflections-on-action through self-selected video vignettes, validation of analyses of their theories

understanding derived from differing methodological approaches. The teachers would participate not only in data collection but also in data interpretation and refinement. This was achieved in part by teacher group meetings at the end of each stage. An overview of the three stages is shown in Table 2.1.

Given the overarching orientation toward the improvement of practice we decided to ask teachers to participate who were regarded as committed and capable practitioners in the use of play activities in the reception class. Nine teachers of widely varying experience were so identified by their professional colleagues and local education authority advisors, and all agreed, indeed were eager, to take part throughout the whole of one school year. A description of their teaching experience and the contexts in which they worked is provided in Appendix A.

In stage 1 of the study the teachers were asked to write two narrative accounts based on the themes 'a recent example of good quality play in my classroom', and 'my advice to a new student-teacher on the role of play in the curriculum for reception children', taking account of the whole teaching process, including planning, organization, teaching approach and, if appropriate, assessment. It was assumed that the writing of these accounts would generate indications of the key elements or categories in their knowledge and beliefs about play. The stories were thus content-analysed to identify these. Seven broad categories emerged – planning, assessment, staff involvement, adult role, play, learning, and external factors. Sub-categories were also identified. In planning, for example, these were curriculum, approaches, and differentiation. A full description of this analysis is presented in Chapter 3.

Teachers met as a group to discuss and validate these categories prior to their use as the framework for the design of an extensive interview schedule (see Appendix B). Each teacher was interviewed for up to two hours with the dual purpose of extending, explaining and justifying the emergent themes, and providing, through these processes, the necessary knowledge warrants. These interviews were transcribed and analysed, drawing on the work of Glaser and Strauss (1967), in order to 'reveal categories . . . explore the diversity of experience within categories, as well as to identify links across categories'. This was achieved by utilizing the three-stage process of analysis suggested by Miles and Huberman (1992) – data reduction, data display, and conclusion drawing and verification. What this meant in practice was a continuous process of reading and re-reading of the transcripts to identify categories and sub-categories, in which comparisons of transcripts and categories were constantly made to retain the integrity of meanings and definitions. Indeed this process is often referred to as the constant comparative technique.

Categorization relies on individual interpretation and inference which may be idiosyncratic. In order to guard against this possibility – that is, to enhance reliability – two researchers independently analysed the transcripts before negotiating an agreed interpretation. This was then discussed with the teachers by transferring the emergent categories and sub-categories into a large concept map to provide a clear and striking visual representation (see Appendix C). The teachers discussed, and verified, these categories, in the second teacher group meeting. Here they were also asked to reflect on their definitions and assumptions underpinning four key problematic aspects of play in practice – free play, structured play, independence, and ownership, as well as the relationship between them.

Information on teachers' classroom practices was acquired through cycles of data collection comprising:

- a pre-observation questionnaire designed to ascertain the teacher's intentions for the activity to be observed
- a videotaping of the play activities associated with these intentions, i.e. pupil-focused
- a post-activity interview whilst the teacher viewed the videotape. In this process of reflecting-on-action both the observer and the teacher were free to stop the tape or to initiate questions. The opportunity was also taken in this interview to discuss factors which mediated teacher's intentions and their fulfilment.

This cycle of data collection was repeated on six occasions in each classroom in order to sample a range of activities on different days of the week and at different times of the year. In each case the teacher selected which activity was to be videotaped. No formal guidelines were provided for this since it was felt important that teachers be given the opportunity to focus on what was pertinent to them in their individual contexts. The average length of an activity was approximately 20 minutes.

Following each recording session the teacher viewed the material jointly with the researcher and discussed significant events. The video material acted as a catalyst to a dialogue about each episode of play and further exploration of key theories in relation to practice. For most teachers, the video sessions provided an opportunity for them to look at play considerably more closely than was normally possible. One teacher commented, 'Watching it on video is very different to watching it in real life. It's almost better watching it on the video. I can actually see the sand tray and see what he's doing, and also I'm not distracted by what's going on around me.' Although teachers claimed to observe children at play as the basis of their assessments, in reality these observations were often brief and irregular, rather than sustained. For some teachers, therefore, the video material was a rare opportunity for them to observe closely, and without interruption, children's responses to a range of play contexts.

Each teacher's observations and comments were recorded and transcribed for analysis. They were also provided with their own copy of the videotape for additional consideration at their leisure, and any additions or amendments were added as they emerged from teachers' subsequent viewings and correspondence. In total, some two hours of video material was viewed with each of the nine teachers.

The issue of researcher effect is important in any classroom-based research and we were conscious of the possibility that both teachers and children could find the presence of a relative stranger with video camera intrusive. However, this was minimized by the desire of the teachers to participate, the fact that the research assistant was herself a reception class teacher, and the regular series of meetings with the research team and participating teachers throughout the study. In addition, the interviews ensured that a comfortable relationship between the researcher and individual teachers was established prior to the classroom visits. Establishing a good relationship with each teacher was an important aspect of the research and one on which successful data collection depended. There was also concern with the way in which children might react to the video camera. Each video session was therefore preceded by a discussion between researcher, teacher and children where the researcher's presence was explained, where children could explore the video camera and ask questions. In the event, few children appeared to notice the camera after more than a minute or two, and the general perception of both researcher and teachers was that any effect was negligible.

These videotape recordings also formed the basis for the third teacher group meeting. Each teacher was asked to select a short vignette to view which either confirmed or confronted their theories of play. A wide range of activities and contexts were thereby illustrated, both of successful and less successful activities, which generated substantial interaction about issues underlying, and mediating, practice. All teacher group discussions were, with the teachers' permission, tape recorded. These recordings, and those of the post-activity interview, were transcribed and analysed in the same manner as the earlier interviews.

Throughout the data collection and analysis process, validity was a constant concern. Consequently, the necessity for warranting knowledge was built into the research design, by requiring teachers to provide reasons and justifications for their theories and their actions. At the level of analysis, descriptive validity – the factual accuracy of accounts – was attained by returning transcripts to the teachers for checks on accuracy (Maxwell, 1992). In order to attain interpretative validity all interpretations, whether in the form of concept maps, or as individual interpretations of teachers' theories, were either discussed by the group, or by the individual, as appropriate, for agreed accounts to be reached.

These analyses are presented in the following three chapters. Chapter 3 details teachers' theories of play, followed in Chapter 4 by an analysis of the relationship of these theories to classroom practice. Chapter 5 then presents three extended case studies to highlight in more detail these relationships, as well as to exemplify the nature of the changes in theories and practices experienced by the teachers as a consequence of their involvement in the study.

CHAPTER 3

TEACHERS' THEORIES OF PLAY

INTRODUCTION

The commitment to a play-based curriculum, a central tenet of the ideological tradition, appears to be based more on rhetoric than on sound pedagogical reasoning. Critical questions about the rhetoric–reality divide are not explored in any depth and the debates about the place of play in the early childhood curriculum are rarely informed by knowledge of what teachers do and why. It is thus unclear how teachers' theories influence their practice, and what factors mediate this influence. The focus of this chapter is on revealing teachers' theories of play and the relationship to their general teaching orientation.

In the first stage of the study, the teachers were asked to write two narrative accounts which were then content-analysed to identify the key elements or categories in their knowledge and beliefs about play. These categories were validated by the teachers, and then informed stage 2 which consisted of in-depth, semi-structured interviews. These data were again content-analysed in order to reveal patterns and layers of understanding, while maintaining the integrity of teachers' meanings and definitions.

The teachers' theories of play and their influence on their general teaching orientation are represented by a concept map (Appendix C). Their theories are remarkably similar, though not uniform, and could be argued to constitute a shared discourse. They are represented on the concept map by six key interconnected areas which show how learning, the nature of play, the role of the teacher, curriculum organization and planning, the assessment of children's learning and the constraints which mediate theories and practice are defined and linked. These areas are not discrete and there is considerable overlap between them. The remainder of

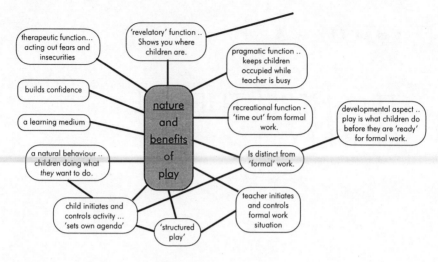

Figure 3.1 The nature and benefits of play

the chapter is structured around these areas, each section representing one area.

KEY AREA 1: PLAY AND LEARNING

Play is regarded as both special and vital in early years education and, in broad terms, there are clear views about its defining qualities and what it does for the child (see Figure 3.1). These are indicated by the teachers' theories within this key area:

- Children's ideas and interests are central to play.
- Play provides the ideal conditions in which to learn and enhances the quality of learning.
- A sense of ownership is central to children's learning through play.
- Learning is more relevant if it is self-initiated.
- Children learn how to learn through play.
- Children are more likely to remember what they have done in play.
- Learning through play happens easily, without fear and without erecting barriers.
- Play is natural – children are themselves.
- Play is developmentally appropriate – children know intuitively what they need and meet those needs through play.
- Play enables children to explore and experiment.
- Children cannot fail in play as there are no rights or wrongs.

• Play enables teachers to observe real learning.
• Children experience less frustration in play, which reduces discipline problems.

The view that play is a vehicle for learning is strongly endorsed by these theories. The defining quality of play is that it is initiated by children and is based primarily on their needs and interests. Children know intuitively what they need and can automatically meet those needs through play. Child-initiated activity leads to choice, control, ownership and independence. Because play is enjoyable, it enhances interest, engagement and motivation. Play therefore provides relevant and meaningful experiences and leads to learning. There is a common concern with children's attitudes towards learning as much as what is actually learnt. Thus play fosters positive attitudes towards learning which help children to develop self-confidence and self-esteem, become more independent and take responsibility for their own decisions.

Beliefs about the defining quality of play as child-initiated activity, and work as teacher-initiated, are held uniformly by the teachers. However, they conceptualize child-initiated activity in a variety of ways. Two teachers describe children 'setting the agenda' in play in contrast to teachers setting the agenda in more formal activities. Most teachers agree with the importance of children 'taking control' and 'being in charge' of their learning, again implying teacher control in other activities. This is covered in more detail in key area 2, since the question of control and ownership related significantly to the teacher's role.

Giving children ownership and control demonstrates that the teachers value and respect children's ideas and interests. One teacher emphasized the importance of this: 'so just on a self-esteem level it's important, otherwise you're saying "I'm the controller of everything that goes on in this classroom".' Many of the teachers felt that children did not have the same degree of control in formal activities. Therefore the contribution which play makes to children's learning is qualitatively different and can enhance learning through a higher degree of motivation and interest.

The importance of 'making children self-sufficient, self-reliant and independent, and making them responsible for their own decisions' was of high priority: 'the sooner the children can become independent and self-reliant, then the sooner they can work for themselves, by themselves,' said one teacher. There appear to be two reasons for this emphasis on independence which relate to the educational and pragmatic functions of play. First, independence is seen as an important life skill which contributes to children's self-esteem and competence as learners. The degree of independence generated in play is equally important in other areas of school life. Second, children need to become independent so that they do not interrupt the teacher, or as one teacher put it, are not 'crowding round her'. So teacher dependency is discouraged as a managerial strategy:

> I think it is important for me to be able to say 'can you get ready to go to Assembly?' and not to have to shepherd them into the hall.

> Play is better for me as a teacher. I'm not sitting on this huge, noisy rabble that I have to control and have to drum to.

Clearly there is a tension between these two functions. On the one hand, teachers value play in its own right, with all the presumed potential benefits that accrue to children's cognitive and social development. On the other hand, children have to be able to play without the teacher's support because of other demands in the classroom.

The theory that children know instinctively what they need is commonly held. These needs and interests lie at the heart of play and are reflected in the choices the children make, their behaviour and actions. This is particularly true of free play where relatively few constraints are placed on children's choices. In structured play, the choice is often limited by the teachers with specific intentions in mind, but is still dependent on the child's rather than the teacher's perspective. Thus even structured play retains some element of choice so that the children can determine the outcome to some extent. In contrast, formal teaching activities are based upon the teachers' interpretations of both curriculum requirements and children's academic needs.

The teachers talk frequently about children learning 'at their own level' in ways which are 'developmentally appropriate'. 'Whatever the children are doing is matching their emotional, intellectual and social needs, because otherwise they wouldn't go to a particular activity,' says one teacher. Children's behaviour in play activities is then interpreted in the light of these theories. For example, one teacher justified a child's repetitive behaviour in the water tray as 'doing what he needs to do'.

Underpinning much of what the teachers say about play is the assumption that it is the child's own natural way of finding out, the way children would learn if they were 'left to their own devices'. Several teachers state that learning must come from within the child rather than from without, suggesting that learning and development are innately patterned, that there are moments of readiness, and that children need play as a precursor to formal work. In this sense, the teachers indicate that their own teaching cannot contribute to children's learning and development in the same way that play can and, in their view, does. There is an underlying belief that 'accurate match' between the child and an activity is determined more successfully by allowing children to follow their needs and interests. In teacher-directed activities, the teachers determine what individual children need to learn, both in terms of their curriculum entitlement and their academic progress. Here accurate match becomes problematic as children may not be interested, motivated or ready to learn in more formal situations. By working at their own level, children can fulfil their individual needs, so play is likely to be more meaningful and more relevant than teacher-directed activities and supports 'quality learning'.

This dilemma between the value of child-initiated and teacher-directed activities is illustrated in the accounts of two teachers which demonstrate the overlap between the key areas of play, learning, assessment and the teacher's role. One teacher explained that since the introduction of the National Curriculum, there was pressure to do more 'formal work' in order to collect evidence of learning and achievement in each of the subject areas. A second teacher felt pressured to collect evidence for other interested groups such as parents, colleagues and inspectors. In order to fulfil these requirements, they considered that the best evidence comes from 'formal work' even though children may find this onerous, difficult and inappropriate to their needs and interests. But from the teachers' theories of play, it is evident that they believe that formal work does not always result in quality learning, whereas play does. Thus teachers apparently have to choose. Either they encourage quality learning through active play which yields little evidence of learning in the way that formal written tasks do. Or they opt for formal work which sacrifices the quality of learning, in which case the evidence is unreliable.

In reality the choice is not based on clear-cut value judgements about the relative merits of play and teacher-directed activities. There is an assumption that accurate match is achieved through curricular self-choice and that going with the child, at his or her own level, is likely to elicit a better response. However, although play is considered to have an educational function, its relationship to learning tends to be specified in broad, general terms with an emphasis on processes such as exploration, discovery and experimentation, rather than content. Play is seen as contributing to the all-round development of the child – physical, intellectual, emotional and social, based on the theory that play is such a natural activity that it is how children would learn if left to themselves:

> Play is essential for the intellectual growth and social adjustment of the child.

> I believe that play, with all its wonderful opportunities, can be used to make children independent thinkers.

Play is seen as 'developmentally appropriate' and as having a revelatory function which 'shows you where children are' and enables teachers to observe 'real learning'. Play is considered to be non-threatening as there are no rights and wrongs and no risks of failure. It enhances the quality of learning and promotes positive attitudes towards school, thus resulting in immediate and potential long-term benefits to the child. However, there is less clarity in the teachers' theoretical understanding of exactly what children learn through play. This relates to the pragmatic function of play. It keeps children occupied whilst the teacher is busy usually with more formal work.

The teachers' theories of play indicate that they undervalue their role. This is underlined in the theory that learning through play is largely incidental and leads to unplanned developments, which implies a passive rather than an active role for the teacher. A number of pedagogical and curricular implications flow from how teachers conceptualize their role.

KEY AREA 2: CONTROL, OWNERSHIP AND THE ROLE OF THE TEACHER

The majority of teachers share the view that the most valuable aspect of child-initiated activity is in enabling children to make choices and decisions, to exercise control over their own learning and, as a result, experience a sense of 'ownership' (see Figure 3.2):

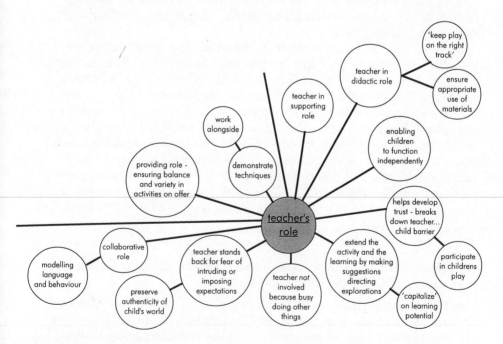

Figure 3.2 Control, ownership and the role of the teacher

I think it is quite important for children to have their own space, their own control because if they didn't that would mean I was taking their ownership, their control away.

. . . play is open-ended. Children make up their own rules, they're highly independent when they're playing freely.

Theories about ownership are so prevalent in their shared discourse on play that the teachers were asked to explain further what was meant by this, and how it contributed to children's learning. Several teachers link ownership directly with self-confidence, motivation, the development of self-esteem and a positive self-concept. It is precisely because play enables children to follow their own ideas that they can achieve a sense of ownership and are motivated to learn. Thus ownership relates to many elements of the teachers' theories about play and learning and is seen as having beneficial effects as children are more likely to develop positive attitudes to learning and to school. So through play children learn how to learn, which is a precursor to later, more formal learning.

In order to promote high quality learning, children need to engage with their environment in an active, exploratory way and the practical, concrete nature of play enables children to experience and control materials, thereby laying the foundations for later, more 'abstract' learning. Play allows children to take risks without fear of failure and to learn through trial and error. These theories have a direct influence on the teacher's role in play, which is characterized predominantly as non-interventionist, though not as totally *laissez-faire*. The teachers' descriptions of their role in play fall into three main categories: provider, observer and participant. Each one is discussed in turn, although they are interrelated.

Teacher as provider

Providing 'a stimulating environment' and ensuring that 'there's a balance and a variety in all the activities that are on offer' were identified by several teachers as key aspects of their role. The provision of resources was remarkably similar in each setting and included sand, water, small world and construction play, a role play area and various table top activities such as puzzles and games. Accessibility of resources (on a 'self-servicing basis'), provision of a wide range of experiences, and timetabling regular opportunities for play were features of the curriculum for all the teachers. Play was planned intentionally into the curriculum, with resources reflecting the current topic or theme. However, planning did not always include specific learning intentions and outcomes as some teachers believed that they did not always need to plan specifically for play because of its spontaneous nature and intrinsic motivation for the children. The provision of an appropriate environment was informed to a considerable degree by their theories about helping children to become independent, to 'take responsibility', 'make choices' and 'exercise control' over their learning. Similarly, creating a 'stimulating environment' in which children could 'explore', 'experiment' and 'find out for themselves' required teachers to give careful thought to the nature and physical organization of material resources. Thus the teachers' theories about play are manifest in their curriculum planning, classroom management and organization.

Teacher as observer

Observation is regarded as an important tool for assessment and diagnosis in early childhood education. It is a strategy rooted in the scientific traditions of child development and is based upon an assumption that externally observable behaviour can reveal internal development and learning processes. Deliberate and planned observation appears to be highly specific to this phase of education, perhaps because, as teachers demonstrated, they are deeply preoccupied with children's personal and social development and with their general well-being when they first enter school. Observation is a central aspect of the teachers' role because play has a revelatory function which allows them to interpret children's play behaviour, continuously adding to and building upon their picture of the 'whole child'. It provides a 'window into the child's mind' and allows teachers to try to understand 'what is going on inside their heads'. However, the links between assessment and diagnosis are not always clear in the teachers' theories.

Teacher as participant

This category highlights some important issues for teachers which are of particular interest in the light of research studies which have linked poor quality play to the lack of adult involvement. There is little information in the existing literature about teachers' perspectives and their justifications for their level of involvement in children's play.

The teachers were asked to describe the nature of their involvement in play. Several perceived a clear contrast between their role in play, which is seen as 'collaborative', and their role in teaching, which is seen as 'didactic'. This appeared to be such a clear distinction that the teachers were asked to clarify their thinking. One teacher described the role of the teacher as 'chameleon-like', constantly changing from one role to the other as she moved from a play situation to a more formal teaching activity. In her view, a 'collaborative' role was more appropriate to play as it required her to 'get down on the child's level' and 'enter their worlds'. By contrast, the didactic role required her to take control, to be 'the teacher' in a 'responsible role'.

Similarly, another teacher contrasted her 'didactic, controlling role' in teaching activities with a more 'supportive' role in play. She explained how she acted as a 'supporter of children's own ideas' in their play. This meant 'valuing their ideas', 'listening to the child', 'offering freedom', and 'accepting what they can do'. A third teacher described her role as 'quite didactic' in a directed activity, whereas in play, she acted as a 'facilitator' to children's learning. Other teachers were not as explicit about the contrasting nature of their roles, but some distinctions were evident in their accounts. For example, one teacher said that in play activities she would 'make supportive comments' but 'try to take a back seat'. In contrast, a teaching activity was 'not an open discussion'.

When teachers talk about the nature of their involvement and how they might intervene it is almost always in terms of 'sensitive intervention', particularly in role play. Some teachers mention that they needed to be 'unobtrusive', to 'stand back' and to 'avoid interference'. They are genuinely concerned that their untimely interventions might 'spoil' or 'intrude on' children's play. One teacher describes this as 'doing the big teacher bit and taking over the play' or 'going in with your size tens'. Similarly, another teacher states that she avoids intervening in play wherever possible, since she regards it as 'their space, their control' and is anxious not to interfere with this. However, some features of the teacher's didactic role are evident in play as they 'ensure the appropriate use of materials' and 'keep play on the right track', so it is not always a totally *laissez-faire*, unstructured activity.

Some teachers do not regard their involvement as essential to the quality of learning in play. This links directly with their theories about ownership, independence and control. One states that the children would 'get something out of it [play] whether the teacher's there or not'. Such comments highlight the belief held by several of them that the true value of play is inherent in the act of play itself, rather than resulting from their involvement. One teacher asserts that 'it would be very arrogant to think that the child is just learning wonderfully because you are there'. Occasionally, teachers will intervene with a specific intention such as 'the teaching of a skill' or to 'demonstrate a technique'. Such interventions are based on children's limitations and the teachers consider it acceptable to model language and behaviour if they became frustrated. However, they do not necessarily regard situations of this kind as play and consider that the teaching input might contribute or enhance play subsequently.

The teachers were keen to preserve the authenticity of children's ideas, which they valued highly and which they believed acted as a motivating force in the learning process. So, wherever possible, they avoided 'imposing' their own intentions on children, thus changing or even 'curtailing' the flow of the play. Several teachers also 'took a back seat' to enable children to 'discover for themselves'. One teacher asserted that 'there's an awful lot of time when you have to stand back and let children just experiment and explore for themselves'. Another teacher adopted the practice of deliberate non-intervention in play settings, so that children could 'find things out for themselves' before engaging in more structured activities with the teacher. As she said, 'They're learning things completely by themselves, through trial and error.' Teachers' perceptions of their involvement in play are influenced to a considerable extent by their theories about play and learning. Underpinning their concerns is a consistent commitment to giving children control and 'ownership' of their learning: 'adults . . . avoid interference . . . [so that] children have "ownership" of their play and take it where they want it to go.'

Involvement in role play

The practices of 'sensitive intervention' and 'non-intervention' are particularly relevant to children's role play, where teachers are most reluctant to participate. Even those teachers who claim to play a more active part in other play activities state that they are less likely to intervene in role play on the grounds that it might 'inhibit' children. One teacher was prepared to intervene if a child was seen to be struggling or 'getting frustrated', and others spoke of intervening in order to check inappropriate behaviour or ensure the appropriate use of materials. However, there is less emphasis on intervening to extend learning or assess processes and outcomes.

Role play is regarded as special and, as such, stands apart from other forms of play. It appears that the learning taking place is less tangible than say, play in the water tray, and is more likely to take off into unplanned developments. Also, when teachers talk about 'entering' into play, or the child's world, they are usually referring to role play, and when they observe and interpret children's play behaviour it is often in a role play context. Not all teachers 'stand back' from this type of play. Two teachers regard role play as an opportunity to interact quite intentionally with children, extend their language use and directly influence the course of 'the plot'. One teacher regards learning through play – including role play – as a 'joint venture' between herself and the children. Interestingly, neither of these teachers utilizes the term 'ownership' in their accounts, and they have fewer elements of shared discourse in common with other teachers. In this sense, their accounts could be described as more pragmatic than ideological and their attitude to involvement is significantly different in this area.

Where the teachers are reluctant to take part in role play, it is often because they are unsure about how, and for what purpose, they might intervene. One teacher clearly felt uncomfortable with intervention – 'it's not something I do myself' – while another stated that 'I don't like to go in the home-corner unless I'm invited'. Several teachers could recall instances when their interventions had a detrimental effect on play: 'sometimes you go in and it's a disaster and you shouldn't have, but you can never judge.' These theories indicate that knowing when to intervene and how to intervene are problematic issues for many teachers. In general, they found it difficult to articulate exactly how they might achieve 'sensitive' intervention and avoid 'imposing' their ideas on children. One teacher describes the dilemma in the following way:

> When thinking about my role, by this I mean how I support children in their learning when they are playing. . . . I have to be highly tuned in to what is going on around me . . . to home in on the possibilities or potential for learning in each situation I observe. I have to be patient sometimes and not leap in; I have to be sensitive to the children's needs – emotional, intellectual, social and spiritual . . . to make time to, and engage in, play with children.

Intuition plays an important part in determining when teachers intervene so that this is undertaken mostly on an 'ad hoc basis', 'spotting a situation', or as one teacher put it, 'seizing opportunities for learning'. The spontaneous and incidental nature of children's learning through play makes it difficult for teachers to plan their involvement. The implication is that anything can happen in play and the real skill of the teacher is knowing how and when to capitalize on learning opportunities and to recognize appropriate opportunities for intervention. However, there is a dilemma here as teachers may not have the opportunity to seize on 'teachable moments' as they arise in play if they are busy doing other things.

The teachers' attitudes to involvement are mainly ideological in orientation and reflect to a considerable extent their theories of play. Thus, their commitment to preserving children's ideas, ownership, the primacy of discovery learning and the spontaneous nature of play shape their role. However, they also give more pragmatic reasons for their approaches. Several teachers are frank about the difficulty of addressing the needs of individual children, integrating play into the curriculum and assessing and evaluating each activity. In this respect, the image of the teacher as 'chameleon' seems appropriate. In reality, teachers are often too busy to intervene in children's play. Several identify the need to attend to hearing readers and teach small groups of children, so that they are not always able to participate in children's play, even when they believe it might be of benefit and value. The apparent contradiction in these two positions – one ideological, the other pragmatic – is difficult to account for. Teachers seem to be suggesting that children learn through the process of play itself and that while sensitive adult involvement may enhance the quality of that learning it is not essential – children will learn anyway. On the other hand, play is used as a means of engaging children in self-maintaining activities while the teacher is busy, which implicitly devalues its worth. It may be that it is precisely because teachers believe so strongly in the inherent value of play that it can be left to the children.

The findings indicate that teachers appear to hold similar views about the nature of play and their role in it. It is evident that the key elements of the teachers' theories about their role give them some control in shaping the play/learning environment with a peripheral role in play activities. Interventions are predominantly pragmatic and managerial and there is less evidence of clear pedagogical intentions. The evidence implies that it is far more valuable for the child to persist with a task and investigate alternative ways of doing things, as learning is likely to be more meaningful:

> I'm loath to do anything for the children [in their free play] because it's their own work . . . I would prefer it to be their own work all the way through. I'm very keen not to say to them, 'That's not going to work'.

This is not to say that the teachers do not support children to help them make sense of their explorations, especially if they are struggling or becoming frustrated. They are quite clear that intervention in such circumstances would be necessary and appropriate. However, the prevailing view is that learning through play involves children 'discovering for themselves', with or without support, rather than simply being told in a didactic fashion. In ideological terms, the teachers' theories are clearly child-centered. In theoretical terms, there is a distinct bias towards Piagetian, constructivist perspectives, which reflects the belief that the true value of play is inherent in the activities and peer interaction, rather than in adult involvement. Thus their theories of play and learning are consistent with their role.

In spite of their strong commitment to play, the teachers implicitly undervalue their role and direct their attention to more formal activities. This reduces opportunities for assessment and critical evaluation of the meaning of play activities to children, and their impact on learning and development. Here the constraints of time, curriculum pressures to teach 'the basics' and adult – child ratios are influential. A further dilemma arose from the common adherence to the idea that play is the child's world, as the teachers did not see a clear role for themselves. They may also lack the confidence and skills for meaningful participation in children's play.

There is a common emphasis on the primacy of discovery learning with varying degrees of curricular self-choice in play. However, it is inaccurate to equate play with a *laissez-faire* curriculum. While there is a general reluctance to intervene directly in children's play, the teachers have a more proactive role in planning the learning environment, formulating learning intentions and organizing their realization through appropriate activities. These are the structural features through which the teachers' theories are translated into practice.

KEY AREA 3: PLAY IN THE CURRICULUM, LEARNING INTENTIONS AND OUTCOMES

As the concept map for this key area shows (Figure 3.3), the teachers' theories about play and learning are translated into practice through the structure of the curriculum, including planning, organization, the learning environment and intentions for learning. They believe that children match their own learning needs through the activities they select, so learning intentions are not always specified clearly and the teachers 'plan for possibilities'. In reality the children's choices are to a certain extent dictated by curriculum organization, the presentation of activities and the provision of resources. This approach ensures balance and variety in the activities offered.

There are three main approaches to planning for play among the nine teachers which will be explored more fully in Chapter 4. First, the High/Scope curriculum model is used, in which the children are allowed to plan what they want to do, carry out their plans, and then review what they have done at the end of a session (Hohmann *et al.*, 1979). Second, the teachers select a range of activities (both work and play) and rotate the children through these during the course of the day. Third, children are allowed to choose play activities when they have finished their work. In each of these approaches, there are opportunities for both free and structured play, terms used frequently in the shared discourse. Free play is usually in the role play area and is related to the ongoing theme or topic. Structured play includes a greater degree of teacher direction as the children might be guided into how to use the materials available with specific intentions in mind. The teachers tend to have broad intentions for all of these activities, with specific intentions for some.

The difficulties of planning for play are revealed by the data. One

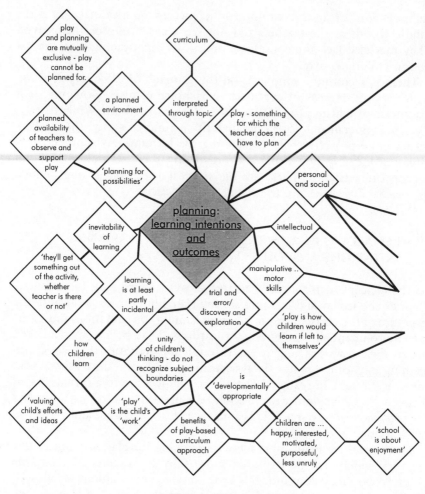

Figure 3.3 Learning intentions and outcomes

teacher believed that play could not be planned for because of its intrinsic spontaneity, but overall there is a tendency to plan for possibilities as well as for specific learning outcomes. The teachers are aware of the broad intentions underpinning the activities they provide, but are prepared to go with the flow of unplanned developments. One teacher described her approach as 'planning for possibilities' by providing a stimulating environment in which children select freely and follow their own intentions. Another teacher likened play to a 'volcano' which 'could erupt into all kinds of things', and where there are 'lots of possibilities'. Another admitted that 'I don't think I'm ever sure what's going to come out of it', but there is a consensus that they need to capitalize on the learning potential which arises from play. Thus they are prepared to extend learning by making suggestions and developing the activity, where appropriate with the notable exception of role play, as noted previously.

The teachers are unsure about the children's potential responses to the different activities provided, but do not regard this as problematic because, as their theories indicate, children's ideas, needs and interests are valued. This commitment appears to militate against clearly defined goals, but supports their theories about children knowing intuitively what they need to learn. This perhaps explains why their planning for play tends to be based more on broad, general statements than on precisely defined learning outcomes. The teachers are aware of the potential for learning which was embedded in different activities, and often resource play to support specific outcomes. However, as will be shown in Chapter 4, because of a lack of involvement, they are unable precisely to define whether their intentions were realized, and what other outcomes resulted from play.

Where learning outcomes are specified, there is an emphasis on the socio-affective rather than the cognitive domain, but it would be inaccurate to portray this as a dichotomy. For example, the teachers emphasize the importance of independence, making choices and decisions, being in control of their own learning, and taking responsibility. These involve social skills, conceptual understanding, attitudes, and the learning of appropriate behaviours, although these fine-grained distinctions are not made by the teachers. The extent to which teachers mention social development is noteworthy, particularly personal skills such as negotiation, collaboration, sharing and taking turns. For all the teachers, play is seen as the ideal context in which children can learn, practise and develop these skills predominantly through peer group interactions. This was consistently evident throughout all three stages of the project.

Play is also seen as a valuable context for encouraging language development and social interaction. When the teachers were asked to specify what they considered children were learning through play, the references were predominantly to these two areas. For example, in language development the children were 'making up stories', 'communicating', and 'using descriptive language'. Social interaction allowed them to 'feel part of the class', to 'see oneself as part of a whole', to share skills and learn from each other. In line with the teachers' theories about children's ownership, there is less emphasis on their own role in these processes and more on the value of interactions between children. One teacher spoke about 'giving children vocabulary', and another of helping to 'extend children's language' through her interactions, but the teacher's role is under-represented and undervalued.

The frequency with which learning is described in terms of children's socio-affective and linguistic development contrasts sharply with the relatively few references to the cognitive domain. When teachers talk about children's cognitive development it was, on the whole, in general terms. For example, one teacher stated that in play children 'pick up . . . lots of basic ideas about life in the real world', and another that play 'extends knowledge and language'. Several teachers talk about learning processes such as problem-solving, and attitudes to learning such as concentration and perseverance. Some are more specific about the potential cognitive content of different play activities. For example, sand and water are related to mathematics, in particular volume and capacity, and to science in floating and sinking, and forces. One teacher talked about 'children experimenting with balance' in a construction activity. Another commented: 'In the sand and water the children are actually doing forces . . . she's worked out that the water will turn the wheel.' Other specific references to cognitive aims include 'counting, sizing, grading and ordering with Play-Doh cakes', 'sorting in maths games such as snakes and ladders and bingo', and 'making sounds in the sound corner'.

In summary, the teachers' planning is characterized by broad developmental aims with an emphasis on the socio-affective domain. Some activities are linked to more specific cognitive outcomes. Interactions between children are valued highly, but there is less emphasis on the teacher's role in play. This indicates some discontinuities between the teachers' theories of how children learn through play and what they learn. Although key processes such as exploration, first-hand experience and discovery are valued, there is less specificity about what the children are learning through the activities provided, even though these processes imply cognitive activity. Some of the play activities lend themselves to more specific short-term aims which can be related directly to subject areas such as mathematics or science. These approaches have implications for how teachers assess children's learning through play.

KEY AREA 4: ASSESSING AND INTERPRETING CHILDREN'S LEARNING THROUGH PLAY

Because play is related to children's needs and interests, the teachers indicate in their theories that it reveals their social, emotional and intellectual development. There is a broad consensus that play has a revelatory function and is a 'good way of showing you where the children are'. Play also reveals the 'unity of children's thinking' which is not necessarily subject-specific and is more in line with their broad, developmental aims. Thus the teachers view play as providing contexts for assessment where they can ascertain a child's developmental stage and their 'readiness' to learn in more formal contexts. In addition, establishing 'where the child is' enables them to 'go with the child' (rather than against his or her natural tendencies) and is likely to elicit a 'better response' (see Figure 3.4).

Several teachers state that in their play, children reveal behaviours which reflect their 'inner needs' and 'deep intellectual processes'. Interpreting these behaviours enables teachers to gain a full picture of 'the whole child'. For example, one teacher stated that a child's behaviour can tell her 'things which have been going on at home' or 'if they are frightened of something'. From this perspective, assessment potentially has a diagnostic function, although from teachers' accounts this is not specified in any detail. In another example, a teacher described a usually quiet and passive child as becoming dominant and much more vocal in imaginative role play. Indeed, several teachers suggested that children behave 'more naturally' in their play and displayed greater language competence. This enables them to assess a child's language ability in play far more accurately than in a formal situation.

In spite of this commitment, in practice the teachers do not appear formally to assess children's learning through play. The methods of assessment which they apply to work or teacher-directed activities are not applicable to play. This may reflect the different approaches to planning for play as opposed to work, in that their intentions are not always clearly defined because they often plan for possibilities or expect 'unplanned developments'. Informal assessments are made mainly through observation but sometimes through involvement. Their availability to do this depends on the amount of time they are able to spend observing and supporting play. In the classes which have adapted the High/Scope curriculum, observation is built into the teachers' intentions for each session and further assessments are made during review time at the end of a session. But this is more difficult for those teachers who adopt a curriculum model in which they are likely to be teaching whilst children are playing.

The teachers are aware of the problems of making time for assessing children's learning through play. One characterized this as 'spinning plates' and others talked about 'keeping half an ear', 'picking up signals', 'keeping an eye', and 'using radar' to assess what was going on in play while they were engaged elsewhere. This element of intuition is prominent in teachers' accounts, but in practice the emphasis is on management and monitoring rather than assessment.

Again the teachers are facing a dilemma because of the contradictions in their theories of play and their actual practice. Most of the teachers believe that observation of children's play can yield important information about their learning and development. Children are able to be independent in their play to a much greater extent than in formal activities, thus at times play is unsupervised and, by some of the teachers'

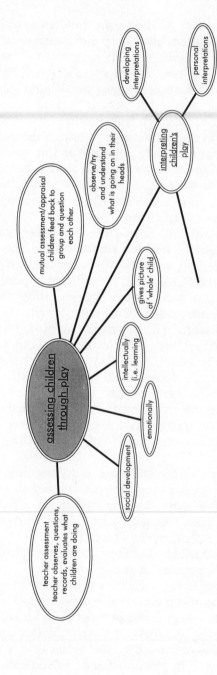

Figure 3.4 Assessment through play

own admission, is often used as a 'holding task'. Clearly if teachers are involved in more formal, teacher-directed activities they are unable to make meaningful and sustained observations of children's learning in play, thus missing valuable opportunities for assessment and for feeding back this information into the next cycle of planning.

Common to all the teachers' accounts is a tendency to interpret children's play behaviour in terms of their personal lives and characteristics rather than learning outcomes. This is consistent with their interests in developing 'the whole child' and their belief that play promotes this in ways that other activities do not. As one teacher stated, 'In play you can assess the sum total of their experience to date.' In many instances, the teachers are preoccupied with personal, social and emotional development. In contrast, few talk specifically about assessment of cognitive processes and outcomes. Where they do, it is generally one part of their assessment of 'the whole child'. The impression given by most teachers is that specific learning outcomes related to conceptual development are better assessed in more formal or structured activities and that the real value of play is that it enables them to observe children in their 'natural state', doing what they need to do in relevant, meaningful ways.

Where assessment through play is carried out, observation and monitoring are common strategies across the group. Another strategy used by some teachers is review or feedback time. This tends to follow on from each session and usually takes the form of a whole-class discussion directed by the teacher. In the High/Scope classes, circle time is a central feature of the curriculum model and is used to allow children to reflect on what they have done or achieved in the session. For those teachers who use a mixed approach (teacher-directed activities alongside independent play), feedback sessions are an important means of assessing 'what the children have done' and 'what they have found out'. Whichever model is used, the teachers generally place great faith in children's ability to reflect on and describe their play. This is seen as giving children the opportunity to 'share their ideas' and to 'feel valued by their peers'. Thus review time has a dual significance as an assessment strategy and a means of raising children's self-esteem through mutual appraisal. One teacher regarded this approach as a learning activity in which children gleaned ideas and information from each other.

The teacher's role during these sessions is to guide the children and ask appropriate questions. However, the children have opportunities to shape the review, to share the discussion with their peers, to take turns and respond as appropriate. This approach is particularly evident in the classes which used the High/Scope model. The skills to participate in this process were learnt quickly by the children on entering schools where it was part of the daily routine and, where they were used successfully, were considered to be effective in consolidating children's play activities. However, there are some reservations about review time regarding the accuracy of children's self-reporting, which will be shown in the following chapter. Nevertheless, review time is valued by the teachers for the opportunities it affords for discussion, showing things the children had made and bringing them together as a whole class.

In summary, the teachers' approaches to assessment reflect their theories about the value of children's play to learning and development. However, some discontinuities are evident in this key area, as they are not always able to involve themselves in children's play as much as they would wish in order to track learning and development. So although there are espoused theories about the benefits of a play-based curriculum, in reality there are a number of constraints which influence what teachers can realistically manage.

KEY AREA 5: CONSTRAINTS

The teachers' accounts and interviews indicate that there are common constraints which militate against translating their theories into practice in consistent ways (see Figure 3.5). First, the demands of the National Curriculum emphasize formal learning and teacher-directed activities with clearly defined learning intentions. Although the National Curriculum is not mandatory in reception classes, this is the predominant form of curriculum organization, reflecting a 'head start' approach into Key Stage 1. There is a need for accountability to parents and other professionals in order to demonstrate curriculum coverage, and provide evidence of outcomes and the children's levels of attainment. As we have seen, obtaining this evidence from children's play activities is not

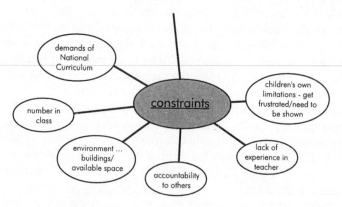

Figure 3.5   Constraints

an easy task, particularly where teachers are unable to liberate time for involvement, or regard play as the child's world, as in role play.

The low ratio of adults to children and large classes also militate against a play-based curriculum. The teachers talk about the complexity of combining child-initiated and teacher-directed activities in these circumstances. They also mention the problem of appropriate resources, space and the limitations of the environments, both indoors and outdoors, in which they work. The mediating influence of these constraints on the differences between teachers' theories and their practice will be explored more fully in the following chapter.

Another mediating factor is the distinction which the teachers make between play and work. Both are valued differently and are considered to have different benefits to children's learning. This contrast was evident in each of the key areas of the teachers' theories and, as such, warrants further exploration.

PLAY AND WORK

The teachers' theories indicate that play is considered to have a special role in learning and is distinguished from teacher-directed activities or work. As we have seen, the teachers value the contribution that play makes to the education of young children to the extent that, in some cases, their teaching was regarded in less favourable terms. The distinctions between play and work suggest that teachers' theories may be characterized as sets of bipolar constructs (Cortazzi, 1993) (Table 3.1).

These constructs are by no means discrete or mutually exclusive. They characterize the similarities between teachers' theories of play, and how it is distinguished from work. As such there is a clear link between the bipolar constructs and the key elements of the teachers' theories shown in key area 1. The motivational force for playing is linked to learning, and 'quality' learning is attributed more directly to play than to work. Accurate match is considered to be more likely through children's self-initiated activity, based on the theory that what they choose to do is what they need. In contrast, work may not be matched to their needs and interests, and therefore does not engage their attention or stimulate intrinsic motivation to the same extent.

The contrast between teachers teaching and children playing reflects the defining qualities of play. Play is seen as being fun and enjoyable, whereas work is serious and even onerous:

> I think if children find it fun and if they're motivated, and if they can set their own agendas for quite a lot of it, I think it enhances the quality of what they learn. I think they remember what they're

Table 3.1 Play and work: bipolar constructs

Play	Work
enjoyable	onerous
child-initiated	teacher-initiated
child-directed	teacher-directed
independent	dependent
children know what they need	teachers know what they need
appropriate	sometimes inappropriate
incidental	planned
unplanned developments	intended learning outcomes
active learning mode	passive learning mode
collaborative teacher role	didactic teacher role
informal assessment	formal assessment
socio-affective outcomes	cognitive outcomes

doing and it just improves the quality of their learning, rather than if I go back to more formal, structured tasks, for the writing and so on. Again they have to have some structure to that quite often, but I would have to say that they find those sorts of things more onerous.

I think play is a non-threatening thing. They all take these risks with the water and so on, and just to take it to a more formal activity say with writing, maybe they wouldn't be . . . confident came to mind, but it's not confident because some of them are confident with their writing, but maybe not take risks so much. They'll come to me and say 'Is this the word I'm looking for?' or 'Is this how you write it?' or 'What does that word start with?'

These comments are typical of the contrast which the teachers make between children's responses to play and work. Most of them make explicit connections between allowing children to enjoy themselves through following their interests and their general attitude and behaviour:

I've found that by allowing children time in the day to plan their own work, they seem cooperative, they seem happy.

If we allow children this time to follow their own interests there seem to be fewer discipline problems, fewer frustrations . . . children are more motivated.

There's much more negotiation, there's much more independence. But when it's a directed thing they do get more tired and their interest isn't sustained in the same way.

Thus work does not foster positive attitudes towards learning or allow the same degree of freedom to explore, experiment and take control of the activity.

It is clear from most teachers' accounts that ensuring children are happy at school is of central importance and is regarded as a key aspect of their professional responsibility:

I think school's about enjoyment as much as anything else.

I think it's so important that children enjoy coming to school and that they really feel, 'I'm going to enjoy it today'.

I try to give everything a game slant, play emphasis, so that they think they're playing.

Enjoyment is seen as an important determinant in the quality of children's learning through play. Teachers recognize that, for some children, entering school for the first time can be a stressful experience. Play provides a link between home, preschool and school and thus helps to initiate children into school routines and norms. As one teacher explained, play is something children know how to do, it is a 'familiar' and 'safe' activity. If play is enjoyable, then they will receive positive messages about school which will enhance motivation. This contrasts with the less enjoyable aspects of formal teaching activities where children may not be ready for sedentary tasks. 'Play is fun,' as one teacher states. 'I think everybody would regard that as fun, whereas quite a few would not regard sitting writing at a table as fun.'

The play/work distinctions evident in the bipolar constructs are reflected in the conceptual marking out of play as 'the child's world' even where it is mapped intentionally into curriculum aims and objectives. This is reinforced in teachers' accounts of their role in play where they talk about 'entering' and 'gaining access' to the child's world. Here children set their own agendas based on their needs and interests. This enables them to be in control of their own learning, particularly in free play, in contrast to more formal activities in which the teacher is largely in control. Almost all the teachers cited this as the most beneficial aspect of play. Thus the teacher's role is predominantly collaborative rather than didactic and there are more opportunities for going with the flow of children's ideas. However, opportunities for adult involvement in play appear to be restricted either by the constraints which mediate teachers' theories and their practice, or by their theories of non-intervention.

Children appear to have more energy when they are playing, and become bored or easily tired in formal, teacher-directed activities. They are more relaxed and confident in play activities to the extent that, in one teacher's view, 'children don't realize they're learning'. In contrast, activities presented in a formal way with technical terms and complex language might undermine children's confidence and actually inhibit their capacity to learn. Again there are implicit messages here about learning being innately patterned, and that it must come mainly from within the child. The levels of enjoyment and motivation in play mean that children are less frustrated, which reduces discipline problems. Thus the play/work divide has a managerial function as it liberates time for teachers to engage in teacher-directed activities such as literacy and numeracy. Although we have presented the play/work divide as a set of bipolar constructs, it is evident from the teachers' accounts that in their general teaching orientation there is some overlap between these two features of the curriculum.

Summary

The teachers' theories indicate that there are strong commitments to play as an integral part of the curriculum for reception class children. Their theories about the nature and benefits of play link directly with their approaches to curriculum planning, organization, and assessment. There is a high level of consensus about what resources and activities should be provided. Underpinning this provision are clearly defined theories about their role which relate to their theories about the primacy of discovery learning and children's ownership and control. The shared discourse indicates that the teachers regard play as contributing to 'high quality' learning because it is linked to intrinsic motivation, needs and interests. Central to the teachers' theories about the value of play is the distinction between play and work. This has emerged as an important dimension among the nine teachers and links to their general teaching orientation.

GENERAL TEACHING ORIENTATION

How was the teachers' strong commitment to play reflected in their preferred teaching orientation? The commitment is such that several teachers stated that if they had the choice they would provide a play-based curriculum based on a 'bottom-up' nursery model, rather than a 'top-down' Key Stage 1 model. In accordance with their theories, they provided a range of broadly similar activities which they classified as play. These included an area for role play, sand and water (and other related tactile media), small world play, a variety of construction equipment and an area for emergent literacy. Some areas such as role play and construction were adjacent to each other but in general there was little overlap between them.

All the classrooms were organized on a self-serving basis so that the children had access to a wide range of materials and equipment. This reflected the teachers' theories about choice and independence, and served the dual managerial function of discouraging teacher-dependency. All the teachers stated that they planned through a topic or theme which usually lasted for up to half a term and play activities were usually related to the current theme. For example the role play area might become a hospital or a post office with relevant resources and intentions for learning. From their accounts it is evident that most of the teachers organized play to run alongside formal activities throughout the day so that in all the classrooms a number of activities were taking place simultaneously. The exception was in the two classrooms where the teachers used a modified version of the High/Scope curriculum model. Here play took place during the time allocated for plan–do–review where children were allowed to make their own choices of activity and the teacher acted in a supporting, extending role. This was referred to as planning or work time, although the terms play and work were used interchangeably.

The children tended to work in small groups, either established by the teacher or self-chosen friendship groups. In spite of these broad similarities, the methods of classroom organization differed so that the ways in which these activities were used by the children, their access to materials and the amount of teacher interaction varied. For example, in the classrooms where children were rotated through a variety of experiences, usually both play and work, the time allocated to each one was determined by the teacher regardless of the ways in which the children developed the activity. In contrast, the High/Scope curriculum model allowed dedicated time for child-initiated activities, although not all of these were classed as play.

In theory, the work/play divide emerges as a set of bipolar constructs. However, in the teachers' approaches to practice, this distinction is not that clear cut. The teachers tried to achieve a balance between play and work, and in some cases there were direct links across this continuum. For example, exploration and discovery were used prior to a more formal input of skills and knowledge. These could then be practised and consolidated further through a variety of play activities. So there are links between teachers' theories of play and how these are enacted through curriculum planning and the range of activities provided. The continuum between child-initiated and teacher-directed activities indicates that play serves different, often multiple purposes:

- as exploration and investigation prior to a teacher-directed activity
- as a free, unstructured activity with little adult direction or intervention

- as a context for developing skills and concepts introduced in teacher-directed activities
- as a context for realizing defined intentions.

SUMMARY

Collectively, the teachers' theories provide a powerful case for play on the grounds that it leads to 'quality learning' through choice, intrinsic motivation, interest and engagement. These theories are instrumental in the teachers' conceptions and constructions of appropriate learning environments. The teachers draw upon theoretical, substantive and practical knowledge based on their personal and professional experience, teacher education courses and personal life philosophies. Their theories have both cognitive and affective content as they are intrinsically bound up with conceptions of childhood and attitudes towards children.

The provision of contexts for a wide variety of play activities reflects key aspects of the teachers' pedagogical priorities. The research approach used enabled the teachers to make explicit and visible the frames of reference they use to shape their practice. The data show that the teachers' theories influence their general teaching orientation through curriculum structures and classroom processes. Thus their theories about play have both ideological and pedagogical orientations. However, although there is a shared discourse about the value of play and its relationship to learning, there are differences in the ways the teachers organize the curriculum which is influenced by their contexts. Therefore, the extent to which their intentions for learning, or their assumptions about learning, are realized through play is a different matter. It has been argued that contexts matter as they can either enable or constrain the enactment of teachers' theories in practice. The model of the hypothesized relationship of theory and action presented in Chapter 2 indicates that there may be a number of constraints which mediate teachers' theories, their general teaching orientation and their actual practice. The next chapter will examine this relationship.

CHAPTER 4

THEORY INTO PRACTICE

INTRODUCTION

Our beliefs concerning teaching and learning will influence our practice whether these beliefs are explicitly held or implicit. They will influence how we behave towards the pupils we teach, how we organize our school and our classrooms and the ways in which we choose to organize our time.

(Raban-Bisby, 1995)

In this chapter we contrast the teachers' theories explicated in Chapter 3 with their actual practice. The model of the relationship between teachers' theories and action presented in Chapter 2 indicates that this relationship is likely to be mediated through teachers' general teaching orientation and their teaching intentions. In turn, the links between intentions and actual practice are likely to be mediated by a range of contextual factors, some of which may be constraining. It is also argued here that teachers' intentions for children's learning, while they may not always be made explicit, are embedded in classroom contexts at an implicit level. In other words, decisions made by the teacher about the nature of the resources and play contexts presupposes some intention. Thus in one classroom the role play area had become a 'hospital' as part of the topic on 'keeping healthy'.

Prior to the observation and video recording of activities in their classroom, teachers were asked to complete a questionnaire about the play activities to be video recorded in order to make their intentions explicit. In this questionnaire the teachers stated their intentions for each activity and gave information about the context, including classroom organization, resources and grouping. They were asked to provide information on the current topic and any background details which might influence the nature of the play. Finally, they were asked to comment on how they thought the children would respond to each activity and how they would know if their intentions had been achieved.

CLASSROOM CONTEXTS AND THE NATURE OF TASKS

Classrooms were generally set up in ways which enabled children to access a wide range of resources and activities independently. Thus the 'self-servicing' approach favoured by most teachers in their interviews, and the emphasis on encouraging children to become independent, were evident in practice. Typically, classrooms were divided into separate areas for different kinds of play, with tables set aside for more formal teaching activities. Thus the distinction made in teachers' interviews between play and formal work was apparent in the physical organization of their classrooms.

Each teacher selected a range of activities which represented a typical day in the classroom. Standard play resources and activities such as sand, water, construction and role play were all well represented, although role play featured more frequently than any other type of play activity. Indeed, with one exception, all the teachers selected at least one episode of role play and many selected two or more. Role play seemed to be of particular interest at each stage of the study, perhaps because, as the interviews indicated, the teachers were less clear about their own role and the nature of children's learning in this type of play. Some teachers welcomed the opportunity to look more closely at aspects of play which were either of interest or of concern. What follows is an analysis of teachers' stated intentions during the observed sessions.

TEACHERS' INTENTIONS

Almost all the teachers' intentions for play were both plural and general in nature. They identified at least two, and often more, intentions for each activity. The general and wide-ranging nature of these reflects the idea of 'planning for possibilities' which was a consistent theme in the teachers' interviews. They acknowledged that play is unpredictable so their intentions incorporated a high degree of open-endedness. There were also many similarities between the teachers' descriptions of the nature and content of their intentions. These similarities can be seen in the following statements in response to the question: what are your intentions for this play in terms of skills, knowledge, and competencies?

Play with construction apparatus
- Group work, cooperation, negotiation, perseverance, concentration, fine motor skills, planning and executing a project, making a structure stable, working to a design.
- Group work, cooperation, interaction, exploration and imagination. Limitations of brick building, children to work together and develop skills of building.

Role play
- For the children to explore the role play area, to negotiate and organize themselves, to create a story line, and adopt roles.
- Cooperation within the group. Develop knowledge of stories they know. Use play to develop story-telling and sequencing ideas.
- To see if the children are able to play in a cooperative way, take turns to share the resources, and take on different roles. To see if their play is of better quality following a visit to a baby clinic.
- Negotiation, language development, responsibility, cooperation.

Small world play
- Cooperation between the children. Can the children place animals in different sets? Knowledge of different animals.

Sand play
- Cooperating, experimenting, generating ideas, constructing, concentrating, problem solving, negotiating, observing, modelling.
- Tactile and route planning, forces – moving sand.

The predominant themes which arise from these statements are the plurality of teachers' intentions and the predominance of social skills. In more than two-thirds of the play activities observed, social skills were stated as the leading intention with cooperation or cooperative play most frequently mentioned. This emphasis is consistent with the teachers' theoretical orientation that play is the primary vehicle for children's social development.

Traditionally, the early childhood curriculum is founded on play and talk, and role play in particular is regarded as an ideal context for the development of social skills, language and imagination. This was reflected strongly in the teachers' theories of play and learning. However, their intentions for role play were almost exclusively social in nature, and made little mention of language development. It may be that as socialization assumes a strong element of language use, the teachers simply did not make special reference to this other than a few examples of story-making and sequencing. After socialization, imaginative play featured most often, although there were few references to the imaginative context, for example, the 'hospital'. There were implicit assumptions that by entering into a role play context, the children would play imaginatively and develop social skills. Thus both the context and the play behaviours would lead to learning.

Several teachers talked about children 'being themselves', being 'more natural' in play than in formal activities, and particularly in role play. But the relationship between children 'being themselves' and 'being in role', and the implications for children's learning were not articulated. In their interviews, they generally agreed that children frequently revealed unknown aspects of their personalities, that they were more confident, and displayed a higher level of linguistic competence in role play contexts. Where teachers' intentions included both social development and imaginative play these were seen as two separate aspects of role play and again the relationships between them were unexplored. Role play presented teachers with some of the most interesting, but challenging, issues during this phase of the study. It may be that they did not fully understand the significance of this type of play other than in broad, general terms.

PLAY AND CHILDREN'S CHOICES

Although there was a high level of agreement in the teachers' interviews about the importance of choice in children's play, there was considerable variation in how teachers interpreted this in their classrooms, and how it related to the organization of play activities. In general the nature of teachers' organization of play influenced the extent and quality of choices available to the children. Three main approaches were identified from the observations of classroom activities, which were explained further by teachers during the post-video discussions. These were:

- Children have total free choice within a structured environment.
- Children are free to play with teacher-selected materials prior to formal teaching input.
- Children are directed by the teacher to a succession of play activities throughout the day.

Each of these approaches is explained in the following examples.

The first approach is exemplified by teacher A who believed that choice is of central importance in play and that it is through developing their own ideas, exercising choice and control, and achieving ownership that children benefit most from play. In her classroom, all the children had opportunities to select freely from the available resources at the same time each day. This enabled her to observe and interact with the children which she described as 'releasing herself' in order to support children's ideas. They could also choose with whom they played but were required to discuss their plans with an adult prior to their play, and to report back at the end of the session in review time.

The second approach derives from teacher B's belief that free exploratory play is a vital precursor to later learning. In practice this meant that children had periods of free play before more formal, skills-based teaching inputs. The teacher selected the materials for the children to play with, and the element of choice was in the doing. In some cases, the choices on offer were narrow; for example, in an art activity there might be only two colours of paint, or clay and a selection of tools. Children were then free to choose what they did with these materials. The teacher did not intervene in their play other than to ensure appropriate use of the materials and to monitor behaviour.

The third approach consisted of a number of different play activities in the classroom through which children 'rotated' during the day. These took place alongside more formal activities in which teacher C was engaged. Typically each session lasted for about 20 minutes, and at the end of the session the teacher stopped the children and directed them to a new activity. The play activities were resourced in line with the teacher's intentions.

Although the teachers offered a consistent theoretical perspective on the nature and value of choice, the observations of their practice revealed considerable variation in the experiences children had of play. Moreover, teachers' multiple interpretations of choice raise further questions about their theoretical understanding. For example, each of the three approaches influenced the ways in which children socialized in their play. In the first approach, children were free to choose with whom they would play, whereas in the second and third approaches the teacher had responsibility for grouping the children. The basis of their grouping included age, developmental level, and the perceived capability of children to learn from each other. One teacher explained how she grouped children for a role play activity:

> The aim is to get the two younger girls . . . to play with Jenny who is the older one and is quite a mature five – she comes from a far more sophisticated and worldly background – and [thus] try and develop their social skills and language skills.

This practice derived from the view that some children may arrive at school with a 'deficit' of experience, that play can take on a compensatory role, and that children learn spontaneously through peer interactions.

In classrooms where children were given more freedom, their choices were often based on social interactions involving negotiation, persuasion and compromise. In these classrooms children were asked in turn to choose what they would like to play with. Although they responded individually, many children engaged in various communication strategies with peers, including body language, eye contact and whispers. One teacher noted this and explained the process:

> A [child] would say that they were going in the [construction area] and it almost became an unwritten, unspoken law that 'oh well, Mark has chosen it, everybody knows that Mark is Richard's friend so he will choose it too.'

The friendship dimension clearly played an important role in how children made their choices and, possibly, the extent to which they sustained their activity. In contrast, where children were grouped by the teacher, there was no opportunity for discussion, and children were unable to negotiate play partners and form their own groups. Although it is outside the scope of this study, it is interesting to speculate on the influence such grouping practices might have on play experiences. Given that teachers' theories tend to emphasize individual interests and needs, it might be asked, for instance, whose interests and needs take precedence in play between two or more children? How do children negotiate when conflicts of interests arise? And what is the impact of peer relations on the concept of choice and on the nature of play itself? These remain relatively unresearched questions.

Other, more pragmatic, factors appeared to influence the choices children made. In most classrooms the teachers limited the number of children allowed in each area as they often needed to guide children's choices to avoid overcrowding. Some also intervened when children repeatedly selected the same activity. As one teacher explained, '[children] can get very locked into being in one area and very stuck in that and there are . . . other equally nice and valid experiences in the class.' Others believed that the choices children made reflected their own needs and interests, and therefore did not intervene. For example, Jennie's case study in Chapter 5 indicates her strong belief that children choose what they need, and sometimes repetition is an important part of that need.

Over half the teachers adopted the approach where children 'rotated' through a series of activities during the day, during which the teacher was usually engaged in a more formal teaching activity. Most children observed in the videotaped activities had far less choice than teachers' theories had indicated. Within this approach, the teachers adopted different strategies for introducing the activity to children and assessing the outcomes of their play. The level of their own involvement also varied quite considerably. Most episodes were described by teachers as 'free play' and, as such, required little adult involvement. There were few examples of teachers being directly involved in play. On the whole, their interventions tended to be of a managerial kind or in the form of brief exchanges in order to assess progress. Nor were there many examples of sustained observation even though most teachers identified this as an essential tool for assessment. Most teachers were engaged in a variety of teaching and managerial tasks – responding to individual children, moving around the classroom or teaching small groups.

In summary, the concept of choice is not straightforward. In each classroom the teachers monitored and guided children's choices in some or all of the ways described above. In some instances, they restricted children's choices, either for sound educational purposes or for purely practical reasons. In their theories, however, a very different and much more uniform picture of choice was presented, where its close association with control and autonomy placed it at the heart of teachers' understanding of play.

INTENTIONS INTO PRACTICE

For several teachers, viewing the videotaped episodes of play was their first opportunity to observe what had taken place. Indeed several commented that they did not know what the outcome of the activities had been. Others had kept 'half an eye' on the activities whilst teaching other groups and had made some observations of what the children were doing. In the classrooms where children's play was reviewed in a whole-class discussion, the teachers elicited the children's views on what they had done. An interesting exercise for these teachers was to compare children's perceptions of their play with the videotaped version of events. There were, perhaps inevitably, some discrepancies. Young children do not always report accurately the sequence and content of their activities and may omit significant moments when recalling events. Children's self-reporting and reflection are clearly of value in terms of reinforcing their language and sharing ideas within the peer group, but their reporting of events is not always a reliable means of assessing their learning.

The videotaped episodes and the teachers' stimulated reflection-on-action provided the basis for the analysis of the relationship between their intentions and actual practice. Some were more successful than others in the extent to which they matched their intentions and actions, but overall about half of all intentions were fulfilled. Fewer intentions were fulfilled in the first phase of the study than in the second, perhaps because, having watched the earlier episodes, the teachers began to change the way in which they organized play and to think more critically about this issue.

Most teachers regarded a successful play activity as one where children appeared to be purposefully engaged and where their intentions were realized at least in part. Given that the teachers usually had several intentions for each activity it was not essential for all of them to be fulfilled by all children. In contrast, a less successful episode of play consisted of children appearing frustrated, struggling, lacking a focus, or even exhibiting unruly behaviour.

The teachers tried to identify what factors had contributed to the success of each play activity. Similarly, where the play had not matched their intentions and expectations they tried to analyse the underlying reasons. In some cases, they were not concerned that children 'did their own thing' in their play, even when they had had clear intentions. Other teachers, however, found that the experience of watching play closely on video challenged some of their assumptions about the way in which children learn through play, how children respond to activities, and their ability to cooperate and interact with each other.

The following examples present episodes where a good match was achieved between intentions and activities. They also illustrate the wide range of responses given by the teachers, and the complex relationship between their theoretical understanding of play, their intentions and their practice.

MATCH OF INTENTIONS WITH PRACTICE

Snow White

In this first example a teacher intended for children 'to role play and negotiate roles between themselves'. She described the background to the activity:

This group [of children] have played quite a lot with myself and the classroom assistant, where we've helped them to think about a story or an idea that they're going to develop, and how to help them think about different roles so that they can talk about it. I was hoping that they'd be able to negotiate their roles and they would play a story.

She observed that

the children decided to play Snow White and they immediately got into roles; Snow White kissed them good-bye and they go off to the mines singing 'hi ho'. They're quite engrossed in this play . . . they're talking about what happens next in the story.

Later she added: 'Through this sort of play I feel they're showing new language . . . helping each other with story-telling and I was pleased with the way they were able to develop the story and talk about what happened next.'

At one point the teacher intervened in their play because:

I've been aware that something has been happening and they aren't able to carry on with their play. They seem to have come to a

standstill . . . I ask [the children] what they have been doing and try
to help them negotiate a new story . . . I decide they've had enough
of doing this activity together and so I give them the opportunity
to go off and do something else. It's very important to be able to
do this.

The two remaining children continued to develop their play, to cooperate with each other, and to sustain their interest in the story.

This teacher stated that her intentions had been fulfilled, and that, in
her view, the activity had been a success. She had given the children a
framework within which to develop their role play prior to the activity,
but had also observed and monitored their progress throughout. As a
result, she was able to intervene and support children when their play
had run into difficulties. Having assessed the situation carefully, she
made the decision not to extend the play except for two children, and
helped them to deal with the problems which had arisen. Although
other groups of children were engaged in more formal activities, this
teacher had decided to prioritize play in that particular session. Thus she
was available to respond to children's needs as they arose and make
some useful assessments of children's development.

Kites

In this example, the children were free to choose from a wide selection
of resources. They were required to discuss their choice with the teacher,
but were free to choose with whom they would play. They negotiated
play-partners and what they were going to play with.

A group of children started to make kites out of paper. One child
appeared to be on the margins of this activity, watching and clearly
keen to participate. However, it was also clear that he was unsure about
how to approach the activity and negotiate access to the group. After
a few minutes, the child approached the teacher and said, 'I need some
help cutting this and I want it to be like David's.' The teacher helped
him to find a space and opened up the paper for him. At first she
showed him what to do, then stood back in order to let him work
quietly on his own. He appeared highly motivated, and deeply engrossed in cutting and sticking the materials. The teacher continued to
observe periodically and stepped in when she saw that he needed help.
At the end of the session, the child took the kite outside with the other
children.

On viewing the videotape, the teacher remarked that the child had
achieved a high degree of success in his chosen activity. She attributed
this to the fact that he had elected to make a kite and that his interest
and attention was generally more sustained in self-chosen activities.
However, his success was also dependent on her support, which she

described in the following way: 'I believe [in] supporting what [the children] do, through facilitating them and trying to stop them getting frustrated . . . so [here] there's some skills teaching . . . how to manage the masking tape because it sticks to other things, it's difficult to cut with the scissors, so I felt that I was doing a bit of that.' She elaborated further on her role: 'It's very much a supportive role, it's completely different from my other role when I'm in a more didactic role, "We're going to learn this today", it's very much, I'm here like your parent or whatever.'

Building

The teacher in this example planned a construction activity with big bricks. She explained how she had recently regrouped children in the class: 'I'd grouped them together as a working group and I am interested to see how they were getting on together – they've only been in these groups for ten days.' Her main intention was for the children to play cooperatively and jointly build a structure. The children were working in an area separate from the main classroom and had a large space in which to play. The teacher's role was to observe and intervene when necessary. She explained why she thought this kind of experience was valuable: 'I think they've got to be able to work by themselves when they need to, work with a partner and as a group . . . [although] I think it's quite a difficult skill.' Unlike her own teaching, play activities, in her view, enabled children to socialize on their own terms. However, she regarded her presence as important in actually 'encouraging the group dynamics and the groupwork to develop'.

The children appeared busy and involved in building, sometimes as a group and at other times in pairs or alone. As the teacher noted, the children appeared to 'plan as they went along'; thus the structure underwent many changes in the course of their play. The end product was not of particular concern to the teacher as she was more interested in supporting children's attempts at working as a group. Her interventions were designed to guide children when they appeared unable to make a decision or when a child seemed to dominate the play.

Watching the videotaped episode supplemented the teacher's perceptions of the activity. She had been present throughout, and was generally pleased that the children had engaged in periods of groupwork with her support. From her observations she was able to make some assessments of how individual children related to their peers and responded generally to the activity. She noted that the children had behaved quite differently in this activity from the way in which they behaved in teacher-directed activities. For example, she was surprised to observe a child whom she regarded as being 'very quiet' organizing children and making lots of suggestions. The teacher commented that they played together 'much better than I expected. I'd hoped that [they would cooperate] but wouldn't have been surprised if they'd found it really difficult.' She added that her presence and involvement had been a key factor in the success of the activity. As she explained:

if I had been across the classroom not watching and doing something else . . . then it could have been a different activity. I can imagine Kirsty wandering off to do something else and David not wanting to come in and getting a bit aggressive.

She stated that her intentions for this activity had been fulfilled and that her observations had enabled her to plan for future activities.

MISMATCH OF INTENTIONS AND PRACTICE

Models

Here the teacher intended children to play cooperatively and make a model out of a construction kit by following a picture. The group of children was directed to the activity after a brief discussion with the teacher. Three of the four children immediately began to build models quite separately and without any interaction. A fourth child was clearly confused by the activity and asked for help from her peers. They were engrossed in their model-making and ignored her completely. She continued to ask for help, but then left the activity. The teacher was not aware of what was happening, as she was busy working with other groups of children.

Later she said that 'adult intervention would have helped [the child]', but also recognized that her intentions were based on certain assumptions about the nature of the task and how individual children would respond. On the task itself, she commented that 'maybe that wasn't such a good intention after all, because if they're following a picture each . . . they can't really be cooperative'. On observing the child who struggled to make sense of the activity she remarked that 'Emma's having real difficulties in making a model, which is quite unusual for her. She's usually quite confident.' Later she said that watching the video 'has certainly focused in on that I've had assumptions about children, maybe I'm thinking that they're more confident than they actually are in some cases'.

Water

In this example the teacher had set up a water tray with toy frogs, rocks and lily pads. The children had visited the school pond and observed tadpoles as part of their topic work. Using the resources as a stimulus, her intention was primarily for the children to develop some joint imaginative play, although she did not explain this to the children. Two children were directed by the teacher to the activity and began to play with the water. At this stage there was little interaction between the children as they pursued their own activity. One child repeatedly pushed rocks into the water, the other poured water from a frog's mouth over and over again. Both were highly engrossed in their activity. At one point the teacher intervened to check behaviour and warn against spilling water on the floor. A third child joined the activity, but this did not deter the others from continuing their play. Eventually, the session came to an end and the children moved on.

When the teacher watched the videotape, she commented, 'They're not making a story, they're exploring the materials . . . they're actually exploring the properties of the water rather than in an imaginative [way] for creating a story.' Although the way in which the children had responded to the task did not match her intentions, she justified it first in terms of their needs – 'they must need to do that. That is probably where they are in their needs' – and secondly, in terms of their developmental level:

> it must be developmental, because John did the same thing with his clay over and over again – he had two large tools and he just kept chopping them into the clay . . . and now all he's doing is pouring water . . . and that's all he wants to do.

In her view their play was valuable even though her intentions had not been fulfilled, since it reflected their level of maturity and had clearly kept their attention.

Post Office

In this role play activity, the teacher stated that she intended the children to 'cooperate, share, negotiate and role play'. Four children were directed by the teacher to the role play area which was set up as a post office in keeping with the current topic. The teacher was busy with another group of children and did not intervene at all. There was little interaction between the children at first, although two eventually formed a pair and began to talk and handle the objects around them. The remaining two children wandered about in the role play area, talking occasionally, but did not engage in any role play activity.

When the teacher observed this episode on video, her immediate response was, 'I'm looking at four completely separate entities who are very busy, but not with each other'. And later, 'there was no role play going on . . . nobody took on any role'. Clearly, her intentions for cooperative play, negotiation and role play had not been fulfilled. When asked to give reasons for this, she talked about the influence of group dynamics and children's personalities: 'if I'd put Jane in there with Katy and if I had Amy in there, then the play would have been completely different. . . . Those children don't seem to need that, or don't like to be in role.' When asked about her own role, she explained that, as a rule, she did not intervene in children's role play: 'I'm not going to impinge on them and I like them to go into the home-corner and do what they need to do. I consider it their space, which is why I don't go in there.'

Wrist-bands

In this episode of water play, the teacher's intentions were social inter-action, colour matching with teddies and boats and imaginative play. A group of four children went with the teacher to the activity where she introduced the activity and explained what she wanted them to do. The children were focused and began sorting the teddies and boats into different colours. Then the teacher left to work with another group of children. The children continued with this activity for a few minutes, then as the teacher observed, 'the play changed'. One child began to throw the teddies into the water. The other children stood back and watched him. He then began dipping his wrist-bands into the water and the others followed. Soon, all the children were engaged in filling and emptying their wrist-bands with obvious enjoyment. The teacher approached the group and talked to them about the teddies and boats. Meanwhile, a child continued to squeeze water from his wrist-bands. The teacher asked this child to 'hang up the wrist-bands' and join in. The teacher said, 'We've got some stones here. Maybe you could use them as an island, or maybe a pathway.' After a few minutes, she and the children began to develop this theme.

In this episode the teacher felt that some of her intentions had been fulfilled, but only as a result of her interventions. The children had interacted and played together, had sorted the teddies and boats into colours, and had developed some imaginative play. However, as the teacher observed, in her absence they were far more interested in play-ing with their wrist-bands in the water. Reflecting on this she stated that 'what they're doing is fairly good. They really are concentrating on their own activity . . . and they're testing the wrist-bands to see how much water they can hold, they're looking at the material . . . they seem focused.' When she intervened, she did not develop this play, as she said: '[The child] wasn't doing what [I'd intended] so I was blanking it out completely and concentrating on the people who were doing what I'd asked them to do.' Thus she did not initially interpret the play in terms of the children's own intentions:

> Not all of my intentions were fulfilled, well certainly not all of the time. [The children] went off on their own tangent and managed to concentrate for quite a long time on what they were interested in, the wrist-bands . . . and that was something I hadn't even thought of . . . the wrist-bands were just there to keep their clothes dry. I tended to concentrate on what my intentions had been and I completely ignored the fact that [that child] was interested in the material. I think you can become quite blinkered.

In spite of her commitment to the idea of children following their own interests, she offered a prescriptive, structured approach to play. Watching the videotape confronted her with a discontinuity between her intentions and what children did, but also raised questions about the relationship between her theoretical understanding and her organization of play. The children's behaviour was easily justified in terms of her theories relating to choice and encouraging children to be 'in charge of their own learning'. Yet in practice the activity was determined largely by her own intentions.

MEDIATING FACTORS INFLUENCING PLAY

The process of reflecting on their practice led the teachers to distinguish between successful activities (children purposefully engaged, teacher's intentions partly or wholly realized) and less successful activities (children appeared frustrated, were struggling, lacked focus, intentions not realized). In their written accounts and initial interview, they identified a variety of structural constraints which influenced the level of success of play activities. These included:

- pressure from expectations of external bodies e.g. parents, inspectors
- lack of adult support
- structure of formal school (timetabling, National Curriculum)
- space and resources
- class size

Attitudes towards the National Curriculum were varied. As one teacher described it: 'You feel that play is important, but the National Curriculum and other demands squash things down, I think. Certainly in reception you get squashed between nursery and the other things going on.' As a result, she identified a gap between 'what you want to do and what you can feasibly do'. This led to feelings of 'guilt' and 'frustration'. Another teacher stated that she could justify her approaches in relation to the National Curriculum. Similarly two of the less experienced teachers in the study felt that the National Curriculum provided a framework which helped them to plan for both teacher-directed and child-initiated activities.

Lack of adult support was a more critical factor which influenced the quality of play, particularly as class sizes rose during the summer term with the third intake of 4-year-olds. Several teachers felt under pressure to teach the formal curriculum, with an emphasis on literacy and numeracy, even when they believed play to be of more value for this age group. In a similar vein, another teacher stated that 'you've . . . got this feeling that you've got things to get through and you plan around what you need to do and there's not that much time for saying, oh that was interesting, let's follow it up'. Other teachers took a more pragmatic stance. One noted that the children 'can't always have an adult doing something with them, and you have priorities, [so] you try to make . . . their time as valuable as possible [by providing play activities]'. It is interesting that for the majority of the teachers in the study, a key element of change was to improve the quality of play through more adult involvement, either in the play itself or by teaching play-related skills, to support socialization in particular.

The ways in which the teachers organized play within the broader curriculum often reduced the amount of time available for observation, assessment and involvement, particularly where they were engaged in teacher-directed tasks. Thus play often functioned as a 'holding' task enabling teachers to teach without interruption. This reflected the dual purpose of encouraging the children to become independent as a life-skill and as a managerial tool. Sometimes, the words *play* and *work* were used interchangeably to give status and value to play for the children and for parents.

In general, the practical constraints identified by teachers were related to their individual classroom and wider school context. Their theoretical understandings of play were more in tune with the preschool phase where there are higher adult–child ratios, fewer pressures and more freedom to teach in ways that are considered appropriate to the age group. However, in addition to these structural constraints, teachers mentioned other factors which influenced the degree of match between their intentions, their observations of play and the level of success of each activity. These included the child's response and group dynamics, the developmental level of the child, and adult involvement and support. Brief examples of each are presented below.

Children's responses/group dynamics

Several teachers related the success or failure of a play activity to individual personalities and group dynamics, as the following comments indicate:

- I'm surprised she's doing this, actually. . . . Normally she would have gone off and found some cutters . . . and a spade or something; that's the type of child she is. . . .
- She'll do her own thing . . . Yes, that's her all over!
- Amy cooperated a lot more with Clair [than I had expected].
- [Quality play depends] on the children in the group, [on] the group dynamics. . . .

Developmental level

- Children are working at where they are, at what they want to do, and it's very difficult to sort of challenge their decisions, because they're still so egocentric. . . .
- [The children] have intentions as well, and they will get out of it what they want to get out of it sometimes. . . . I think you've got to be prepared to accept that, because that's where they are. . . .

Adult involvement

- I feel that play activities are a joint venture between the children and me, where I'm helping them to look at things more closely, and to take things a step further.
- Without adequate adult support, play is probably of a more shallow quality where I am skimming the surface.

DILEMMAS

The data revealed the teachers' perceptions of discontinuities between their theories and practice. These can be characterized as a set of dilemmas which, as Berlak and Berlak (1981) argue, represent the thought and action of teachers as an ongoing dynamic of behaviour and consciousness within the particular context of schooling. In their view, these dilemmas describe the tensions between alternative views, values and beliefs and represent the diverse and apparently contradictory patterns of schooling.

Teachers' role

Most teachers shared the view that children's play behaviour reflects 'where they are', that it is their private world and that they should have 'ownership' of their play. These theories appear to underpin the predominantly non-interventionist approach adopted by many teachers. Yet on viewing the videotaped episodes, some were unable to sustain this position. Two teachers observed that children ignored the role play contexts which they had provided and developed their own themes. In one episode, the children persisted in playing 'babies and dogs', although the role play area had been resourced for a birthday party, and in another, children continually played 'guard dogs and burglars' in the class 'shop'. So taking ownership became a dilemma where the children played to agendas which did not fit comfortably with the teachers' intentions, and resulted in disruptive behaviour for the rest of the class. Each teacher was anxious to raise the quality of children's play, yet they were equally reluctant to intrude, thereby 'taking ownership away'. These observations had challenged some of their theories about play and about their role, in particular the nature of their involvement. They were constrained by their own theoretical understandings of play, which implicitly undervalued their own role. Chapter 5 shows how three teachers worked towards resolving these dilemmas.

It can be argued that many of the teachers' theories were not realizable in practice because of the age and developmental level of the children. They were often expecting the children to operate independently where they did not have the requisite social or cognitive skills to interact productively, follow through their plans, negotiate, play collaboratively or resolve conflict. As we have seen, many of the less successful episodes of play were characterized by a breakdown in social skills or by children encountering cognitive challenges which could only be resolved with adult support. Accordingly they were often making unwarranted assumptions about the value of play, its relationship to learning and about the children's competences.

Management and organization

All the teachers valued play as an integral part of the curriculum, but had different methods of management and organization. Reasons for this were related to some of the constraints outlined previously. One teacher felt under pressure to teach a more formal curriculum and thus gave little time to observing or participating in play. However, through her observations, she identified the fact that children needed support in developing skills, particularly in activities which she had hoped would lead to co-operation and negotiation.

The role of all the teachers was multi-faceted and included overseeing the entire classroom. They frequently described their role in their interviews in terms of 'keeping half an eye' on everything that was going on, of needing to be like a 'radar' and of 'spinning plates'. One teacher summed up these multiple demands as follows:

It's far easier for a classroom assistant to go off with a group of children and get some lovely work out of them, but then they've only got that group to monitor and to think about. Whereas even when you try to work with a group of children, I'm doing clay here, but I'm not, I'm in the water tray. Because you've got to have that eye round the classroom all the time, you've got to be aware of the noises and the safety really.

Similarly, another teacher described her role as the 'general manager', where she was often in a supervisory role and unable to dedicate quality time to children's play.

The ways in which the teachers conceptualized play at a theoretical level often did not match their management and organization. Thus in spite of a commitment to 'ownership', 'freedom' and 'independence', some of the teachers provided a great deal of structure. Whilst this is both inevitable and desirable in a school context, some activities described as play by the teachers were not child-initiated but teacher-directed. This was rationalized by two teachers on the grounds that they wanted all their activities to be more play-like in order to foster positive attitudes towards learning such as intrinsic motivation, engagement, concentration and creativity. It is arguable whether some of the activities could be classified as play, but the teachers' definitions were important in the context of this study. In some cases, there was a clear mismatch between their theories and immediate intentions, but this also revealed the ways in which teachers have to accommodate to everyday classroom realities and constraints.

Alongside broad skills and attitudes, some teachers felt that they had to prioritize curriculum-based content, and there was a distinction between what needed to be taught and what might emerge spontaneously through play. However, in all cases there were some links between work and play, although these were forged more strongly by some teachers. For example, one teacher gave an example of a role play context which integrated learning objectives in literacy, numeracy, technology, leading on to further learning which she described as historical, creative and geographical. Thus how they conceptualized learning, the subject disciplines, and play, influenced their management and organization.

SUMMARY

In this chapter it has been shown that many episodes of play did not match with teachers' theories and intentions. In some cases, teachers' assumptions about how children would respond and what they would learn were strongly challenged. There were also examples of play which confirmed many of the teachers' theories and in which their intentions were realized. In general, these examples usually involved adult participation, or some discussion prior to the play, in which the teacher outlined her expectations and helped children to articulate their ideas.

Some key points can be made, in particular about the discontinuities which exist between teachers' theories, intentions and practice:

- The teachers emphasized social skills in their theories and intentions, but there were few examples of children engaging in cooperative play unless an adult was present in a supportive role.
- Role play continued to preoccupy the teachers, and confronted them with some challenging issues, particularly regarding the extent to which they felt able to intervene without 'taking ownership away'.
- The teachers emphasized the importance of choice in their interviews but, in reality, most adopted an approach in which activities were largely determined by them. The teachers' theories were concerned predominantly with free play, whereas in practice most play was structured.
- The practice of 'rotating' play and more formal activities militated against teachers being involved in play for sustained periods, since their attention was most often focused on formal tasks with small groups. Where play appeared to fulfil teachers' intentions, and where children were described as 'engrossed' and 'focused', teachers were generally available to observe and participate.

In their theories, most teachers adhered strongly to the view that play and learning are interrelated through a variety of processes. These included promoting children's interests, choice and ownership, developing autonomy and control and fostering intrinsic motivation, engagement and concentration. Yet in their practice over half the teachers adopted an approach in which play activities were largely determined by them and allowed for relatively little choice. In general, play was far more structured in practice than teachers' theoretical accounts indicated. For some, the contradictions between their theories and their practice were related to practical constraints such as the management and organization of play in the classroom. In other instances, teachers' assumptions about play and about individual children were challenged. As a result they revised, in some cases substantially, their theories or their practice, or both.

A key issue was their assumptions about their role, especially where it became clear that play was often less successful when teachers or other adults were not involved. In many episodes children were not given guidelines prior to or during the activity. Without adult guidance or intervention it was perhaps not surprising that children played in their own way and according to their own intentions. However, on viewing the videotaped episodes, several teachers commented that children were not doing what they had hoped or expected. This raised some critical questions for teachers and provided the basis on which many began to re-examine and ultimately change their approach.

Several teachers stated that they had made assumptions about the children's abilities to socialize and cooperate in their play, and about how individual children would respond to a task. The view of play expressed by most teachers is based on a common, almost universal, perspective of play and learning in the literature on early childhood education. However, this view is not substantiated by reflection on the nature of individual classroom contexts and, in particular, the nature of reception classes. This raises some significant questions. Can it be assumed, for example, that all children have the skills to play in the way we expect them to? Do young children need help to learn to socialize, to negotiate and cooperate, or is it something that we can leave them to work out for themselves? Do teachers need to teach children how to play? From the videotaped episodes it became clear that children do not always find play in school as easy and natural as the teachers' theories suggest. This challenges the theory that play provides a useful bridge between home and school and enables the children to settle more easily into school norms and routines. Nor is play in school always a 'safe and familiar' activity; it can also involve frustration and conflict, and is constrained by the practical factors outlined above.

Through their involvement in the study, the teachers were confronted with many dilemmas and challenges both to their theories and to their practice. This had the unintended outcome of stimulating change.

Changing theories and practice

The research approach encouraged the teachers to problematize and reflect on their practice. It also stimulated practical reasoning (Fenstermacher, 1994) which acted as a means of transforming the tacit quality of their knowledge to a level of awareness that led to reflective consideration. The issues outlined here and in Chapter 3 became a focus for discussion in group sessions and were confronted openly by the teachers as they exchanged ideas and interpretations. This level of critical analysis led to the unintended outcome of stimulating change in their theories, their practice or both. The nature of these changes varied considerably among the teachers depending on their individual contexts and their responses to the videotaped episodes of play. For most of the group, certain assumptions held about play and learning, and about individual children, were challenged as a result of these processes. Significant areas for change included:

- making time for quality interactions to enhance learning through play
- reorganizing the timetable to allow children extended time to play with teacher participation
- reconsidering the use of ancillary help

- recognizing opportunities for teaching through play rather than emphasizing spontaneous learning
- integrating play into the curriculum through clearly specified aims and intentions; for example, embedding literacy and numeracy activities in play
- teaching children the requisite strategies and social skills for being independent, making choices and decisions
- freeing the teacher to observe, interact and make assessments of the children's learning in order to feed back into curriculum planning.

In most cases the teachers were able to identify where there was a mismatch between their theories and their practice and, as part of the process of change, sought to align these more closely and address some of the mediating factors and constraints in their individual contexts. The following example demonstrates this process.

One teacher believed in the value of free play and the opportunities it provided for children to follow their interests. In practice, free play functioned either as a holding task while she was busy teaching, or as a reward when work had been completed. She considered that this approach implicitly devalued play in the children's eyes and, as a result, it often 'degenerated into messing about'. Her concerns about the poor quality of play were confirmed by the videotaped episodes.

In the process of reflecting on the mismatch between her theories and her practice, she identified several constraints, the main ones being pressure from the National Curriculum and the expectations of parents and school inspectors. Because of these constraints, she felt obliged to provide reliable evidence of children's learning, usually in a written form. Although she believed that play was more likely to lead to quality learning experiences for the children, it did not yield the required evidence.

After a period of reflection and discussion with members of the research group and colleagues at school, she decided to change her practice to include a session each day for free play. This was structured by the PDR (plan–do–review) system derived from the High/Scope curriculum and was referred to as planning time rather than choosing. In her view this structure gave play a focus whilst retaining her theories about ownership, independence and self-initiated learning. Because she was no longer teaching groups, her role also changed and allowed more time to observe and interact where necessary. Consequently, in her view, the quality of play improved and she was better able to articulate and justify what the children were learning. Almost a year later she reported the impact of her involvement in the study:

> I've changed my theory and practice . . . I've gone away from choosing time towards planning time . . . it's upped the quality of what's happening and upped my knowledge of what's happening . . . the

children talk to me about what they're planning. I'm feeling less anxious about making time to observe. I've accepted that other things have to go . . . and if I value it then I have to make the time . . . it means I'm not working with another group on a more formal activity. I may not be hearing readers [but] they are reading to me . . . in the writing area [and] the role play area . . . all those skills are happening, it's just me feeling happy about it.

A key factor in developing the quality of play in their classrooms was changing the organization and management of play to allow for more teacher participation. One teacher described similarly how she had moved away from a 'supervisory role' in which she was the 'general manager'. She had little time to focus on what the children were doing and was exploring ways in which she could share responsibilities with other adults in the room. 'Freeing the teacher' was a common theme and increased participation was justified by another teacher on the grounds that 'by being with [the children] I can enable them to play in a better way. I can extend them in the way I would in any other activity.' In general, the teachers recognized that they were making assumptions about the value of play which were not realised in practice. Often they assumed also that children were operating at a higher level in their play than in formal teacher-directed activities, but again this was not always borne out in the videotaped episodes. There was a broad recognition that they needed to be more explicit about their expectations for play and to observe and interact more in order both to extend and to assess children's learning. The focus shifted towards play as a context for teaching, rather than making assumptions about its value as a context for learning.

There was some reflection on the origins of their theories and their influence on their practice as they engaged in the process of change. One novice teacher explained this clearly:

From my training we talked a lot about Vygotsky rather than Piaget for the subjects. But when it came to play, that was Piaget, it was exploration, child-centred and it wasn't treated the same as other subjects so when I came into my classroom I treated them differently . . . and now I'm thinking to myself, well, I can use the same approach, but it's never been talked about in the same terms. . . . In my planning, I'm going to make sure my learning intentions are clear rather than standing back or being directive . . . it doesn't have to be that extreme.

The processes and outcomes of change differed among the teachers according to their experience and teaching contexts. In the following chapter, the issue of change is dealt with in more depth through detailed case studies of three teachers.

CHAPTER 5

CHANGING THEORIES AND PRACTICE

The following case studies track the processes of change in three teachers with contrasting theories, differing approaches to their practice and different levels of experience. The first shows how an experienced teacher, Jennie, managed significant changes in both her theories and her practice. These processes were underway before the beginning of the study and Jennie's involvement served to clarify and confirm her new theories and approaches. In the second, Eve perceived a mismatch between her aims and intentions in some of the play episodes observed which made her realize that often she was making assumptions about the value of play. She identified aspects of her practice which needed changing, but this was seen as difficult in view of the constraints which mediated her ideals and her actual teaching context. Third, Gina's case study shows how a novice teacher recognized her initial idealism about play and gradually modified her theories and changed her practice.

Each of the case studies is presented as a 'story' in order to preserve the teachers' own words as much as possible and to convey the rich and illuminating nature of the data.

JENNIE'S STORY

Jennie had over 20 years experience of teaching young children. She was extremely well-organized, and was constantly evaluating her practice in order to improve the quality of children's learning. She taught in a large inner city primary school and planned collaboratively with another reception teacher who was also involved in the study. Another colleague had introduced Jennie to the High/Scope curriculum model (Hohmann et al., 1979) which she then researched and used as a framework for changing her practice. Jennie's approach to play was based on a modified version of this curriculum. Most of the children's play took place within this framework, which encapsulated the key elements of Jennie's theories and philosophy of education for young children. As the study progressed, she became even more convinced that this was the most appropriate way to work with reception-age children. The theme of change recurs throughout Jennie's story, reflecting changes in her understanding of how children learn and of her role in work and play, and also changes in her practice.

Jennie's theories

Jennie's overriding concern was with the individual child as an active, initiating, thinking and enquiring learner. This was of central import-ance in terms of understanding the way in which Jennie worked because it underpinned her theories and practice. This concern was related to the key elements of the High/Scope curriculum model which is based on active learning, child-initiated investigation, play and talk, and incor-porates the plan–do–review (PDR) system. PDR time is child-led and, wherever possible, is based on children's ideas, interests, perceptions and emergent understandings. This was perceived by Jennie as one of its major strengths. She believed that children were more likely to achieve what was appropriate for them if they were able to pursue their own ideas, particularly in the context of play: 'I've found that by allowing children the time in the day to plan their own work, they seem cooperat-ive, they seem happy.' In common with other teachers, she saw intrinsic motivation, interest and engagement as central to successful learning and to play:

> I think there are different levels of quality of play, and when engaged in high quality play children appear focused, interested, willing to persevere and intellectually challenged, enabling them to concentrate for long periods.

The PDR system had provided Jennie with a means of enacting her theories about play and children's learning. She believed that 'play offers rich possibilities for learning', 'has a deep intellectual effect', and 'lays the foundation for intellectual thinking'. Jennie's belief that children know intrinsically what they need is linked to the idea that PDR allows children to do what is appropriate for them. She placed great faith in children's innate knowledge of how to fulfil those needs in a particular way and at a particular time: 'Whatever they're doing is matching their emotional, intellectual and social needs. I mean it must be . . . because otherwise they wouldn't go to that particular activity.'

In planning time, the child 'sets the agenda', which distinguished chil-dren's play from Jennie's own teaching. The children are then expected to put their plans into practice, a key element of the High/Scope philosophy which enables them to be in control of their own learning. Jennie believed that through these processes the child 'forges links', 'makes connections', 'experiments', 'initiates ideas', 'practises skills', 'learns to control materials and tools', 'interacts with other people and with the environment'. The latter point is interesting because Jennie clearly believed in the value of social interaction in play. However, in this study she seemed primarily interested in individual learning and development:

> I think [my approach] is about meeting individual needs . . . it's about taking account of how young children learn . . . in an ideal world you would have the things and the adults to support them, I think it would be idyllic. . . . But as it is, because of the situation that we have, we have to group them together, like-minded ability, like-minded stage of development.

Like Gina and Eve, her theories revealed some tension between her ideals and her real situation. However, the PDR system at least allowed her to get close to her ideals and she reiterated her belief that because the children were 'setting the agenda' the activities would be 'developmentally appropriate'.

Jennie's interest in individual children was demonstrated most clearly in her preoccupation with 'schemas', which are defined as patterns of learning and are manifest in individual behaviour. Her interest in schema theory derived from her reading and discussions with other teachers, and was based in particular on the work of Athey (1990). She was unable to articulate a clear definition of what a schema is, but clearly believed that they were highly significant in terms of children's learning. Many of Jennie's stated intentions for children during PDR time were schema-related; from this follows her preoccupation with trying to make sense of children's repetitive behaviours and their persistent concerns, which she believed revealed something about their deep intellectual processes. This concern with the cognitive dimensions of play is a recurrent theme in Jennie's data. In her account of a good quality episode of play, she described how Erin made a puppet during PDR time. The significance of this was interpreted in relation to Jennie's theories about schemas and independent learning:

> I felt it was an important episode of play because it marked the beginning of a transition for Erin from being dependent on me for ideas, emotional support and technical help to becoming independent, confident and able to tutor others.

Jennie had gradually become 'much more interested in the children's own perception, their own ideas'. She saw this approach as much more in keeping with children's experiences in the home, and one which allowed a 'natural approach' to educating young children with more freedom. Jennie believed that learning is always partly incidental, and occurs through trial and error, so her approach worked with rather than against the child. She felt that her practice was now more 'developmentally appropriate', which had positive benefits in other areas. So, by planning their own work, the children were 'happier, more willing, better behaved . . . no longer a huge noisy rabble'. This, in her view, contributed to the quality of learning and interaction as the children were more motivated and in control of their own learning.

Although Jennie emphasized the primacy of children's needs and interests as central determinants of the choices they made, a point of conflict emerged during the first interview. She admitted to having a problem with 'super-hero figures' such as 'Batman', so there were times when she had to limit their choices and make them more 'educationally sound'. This implied a value judgement based on her own perceptions that some forms of play are more educationally worthwhile than others. This tension will be explored further in examining Jennie's theories in action.

Teacher role

Jennie believed that her role was to support children in their learning when they were playing, which meant that she had to be highly 'tuned in' to what was happening, and the potential for learning in each situation. Like Gina and Eve, she felt that she had to be patient and 'not leap in', and be 'sensitive to the children's needs – emotional, intellectual, social and spiritual'.

Changes in practice had inevitably meant a change in role for Jennie, and she was articulate about the different levels of involvement she had in children's play. First, she saw her role as that of a provider of opportunities and appropriate resources for children's play. She planned so that there were 'possibilities for different kinds of learning' and tried to ensure that whatever children needed to pursue their interests was available to them. This was quite a complex process as children's emergent needs and interests had to be followed up on a weekly basis. Second, Jennie was free at PDR time to observe and, where necessary, support children's learning. This was critical in order to keep track of children's interests and schemas. The notion of 'supporting' children meant that she did not intrude on their play or impose her own ideas on what they were doing. This enabled her to respect and preserve the 'authenticity' of the child's world, an idea which was central to her beliefs.

She felt reluctant to intervene unless the ideas were 'coming naturally from the child' as this seemed to 'work against or shut down any kind of ideas they had in their own mind'. However, in play she was open to tuning her responses to the children's schemas or patterns of learning. In contrast, Jennie would engage in direct teaching through small-group time, often beginning with brain-storming sessions which then informed her planning. She felt that learning processes were important but recognized the need to teach knowledge and skills in meaningful contexts.

It is interesting to note that Jennie felt more 'intrusive' in children's role play and, as a result, rarely involved herself in it because 'I think I feel that I'll be an inhibiting factor in that kind of play'. She felt happier if she was invited in to the role play and clearly had some difficulties reconciling her own intentions with the children's. However, as will be shown in the section on Jennie's theories in action, she was open to changing her theories on this aspect of her role.

Although the focus here is on PDR, Jennie's own teaching (small-group time) and the High/Scope approach actually worked together to form a coherent approach to planning and assessment. She described the key elements of her practice in the following way:

> there's the complete freedom [in] the plan–do–review kind of play and I'm there and if the child needs me I'll step in and then there's the small-group time . . . when I'm directly teaching certain skills, processes, concepts . . . and then there's the sort of half way where there's a bit more freedom but I'm stepping in and I'm going to use what I've seen and heard to actually influence my teaching.

Thus her role changed in each activity, but there were clear links in terms of learning and content. Jennie defined her role in teacher-directed activities as being distinctly different: 'I think I'm more didactic . . . I have an agenda.' In contrast, the role of the adult in play was essentially flexible and open-ended and included giving practical help where necessary, facilitating further exploration, helping children to make sense of their experiences and building up a picture of the whole child. Jennie did recognize that there were opportunities for direct teaching during play, depending on the context, and was comfortable with this approach where it was responsive to the child's intentions. These strategies were seen as helping to improve the quality of play by giving support for children's own ideas. Jennie was able to use her observations of children's learning and their schemas to inform her planning:

> Erin's persistence in exploring people and coverings involved all of us in the related topics of masks and uniforms as well as providing opportunities for exploring curriculum-related themes such as early experience of area, ordering (when he made a washing line), moveable joints (on robots) and the need for refining methods of joining (technology).

Jennie could see clear benefits in her new approach and, as a result, she felt that her theories and personal philosophy were being realized far better in practice. However, she continued to reflect upon what she was doing, to question her approaches, and was open to learning through these processes.

Assessment

Jennie tried to plan time to be involved with children's play as much as possible, or directed other adults to take on this role. She assessed the children through observation and interaction where possible, but mainly during review time where they reported on what they had been doing. This was seen as particularly valuable for several reasons:

> I have a structure for rotating myself around these groups so that I get to review with all the children at least once a week (this is when numbers are large) and my colleague, parents and classroom assistants report back verbally anything of interest which came up in review. If I am on my own with a large group I try to link ideas together and explore these with the whole group . . . I am also alert to the potential of follow-up, either in small-group time or another PDR session.

So assessment was seen as an integral process which fed back into the cycle of planning and provision:

> I would try to think of ways to support and extend learning, maybe teaching specific skills, providing alternative material, teaching a new song and generally helping the children to make links. Children are wonderful initiators of ideas and there never seems to be a lack of potential for follow-up.

She did not plan for assessment, but responded to 'whatever I feel is significant'. However, she felt that play offered opportunities for gaining 'a much better picture of the whole child's intellectual, emotional and social development' and 'the sum total of their experience to date'. Jennie was able to assess the National Curriculum subjects through play activities because of the 'exploratory, investigative emphasis' in maths and science, and by incorporating 'a strong emphasis on literacy through play'. However, she was aware of the breadth of assessment needed at this age and she linked this process with her understanding of schemas: 'When children are playing I'm looking for repetitions of behaviour or particular interests that are manifesting themselves in what children are doing.' Her account of a good quality episode of play indicated that she was able to evaluate her approaches critically:

Was I to let Erin continue or should I suggest he try different activities? Was his dogged persistence in, say, staying with the puppet making for six days denying him access to a broad enough curriculum? What was this strong need in him which always brought him back to making people or clothes? What help beyond the purely technical could I give to Erin to support his learning?

These questions were both practical and pedagogical and typified Jennie's reflective approach and willingness to challenge her ideas and her practice.

General teaching orientation

The High/Scope curriculum model provided a structure through which Jennie could enact her theories of play. Her approaches were clearly thought through:

> Given that I feel play is a valuable vehicle for learning, making sure children have equal access to support when they are exploring their own ideas through play, plus effective monitoring on my part, including feedback to parents, give me the greatest professional challenge.

She held clear ideas about how to organize the learning environment and plan the curriculum, and the role of teachers and other adults. The curriculum was planned around a topic each half term and she involved children in making decisions about the role play area, organizing the learning environment, and making props and resources. She felt it was important to offer children first-hand experiences 'as this always enhances play and encourages authenticity'. Jennie's approach to planning for possibilities was consistent with her theory that 'children seem to need to follow their own ideas'.

In line with her theories about independence and autonomy, the learning environment was organized to provide open access to resources with all equipment labelled, and 'a system for matching equipment back to its storage space with the use of illustrations or silhouettes'. There were specific areas devoted to, for example, writing, maths and technology, but the children could 'blur the boundaries' in their play and use resources from different areas: 'We've got a maths and science area, so even though the children might be playing when they're in there, there might be a scientific or mathematical slant to the play.' This also ensured that the range of activities available was linked mainly to the core areas of the National Curriculum and she stated that 'I can justify what I'm doing in terms of the National Curriculum'.

In the PDR system the children were allowed to plan their own activities but these could be categorized as either work or play – the distinction between the two was not always clear. It appears that the words play, task and work are interchangeable, but all shared similar features of motivation, interest and engagement, and all encouraged independence and autonomy. 'I will explore these ideas with them further and ask what they think they are doing or which area they will work in. I may . . . work with a particular child once I have observed what is happening.' Jennie encouraged the children to refer to work or planning time, but was happy if they used the word play for interesting reasons:

> I tend to use the 'plan' and 'work time', because I believe that their play is their work, and play hasn't got a very good press. So if the children can see it in terms of work, and that message then goes home to parents, I think that's helping to raise the status of play by calling it work.

Jennie also made links between teacher-directed and child-initiated activities by bringing in different stimuli connected with the topic. This had a beneficial effect:

> Children have begun to take on this role of initiators of ideas for play themselves, often bringing in materials from home. Again, this is highly motivating for themselves and others engaged on their task, as well as raising self-esteem as their ideas are valued.

Children's ideas were seen as the starting point or 'springboard' for finding out where they were, which then informed curriculum content. At the same time, play was structured to incorporate specific learning intentions, particularly in literacy and numeracy. Jennie was not always able to engage with children on their self-initiated activities, but would direct other adults in the classroom to give support when they were available. She used review time as a means of assessing and evaluating what the children had done.

Constraints

For Jennie, the National Curriculum was seen as a constraint because of content overload. Nevertheless, she was able to work in the ways she thought appropriate for this age group, with the support of the headteacher, who valued the early years. Thus she accommodated her practice to the National Curriculum using elements of the High/Scope model. Class size was also an issue, particularly in the summer term as the third intake of reception children into school pushed numbers to over 30. She felt that this system was unfair to summer-born children who had the shortest time in school with the largest numbers in the class.

Jennie felt that, in order to implement PDR effectively, she needed more adults in the classroom. Review time was seen as particularly valuable for encouraging the children to feed back their ideas and reflect on their learning, but she was unable to give this enough time, to give children equal amounts of time or to teach them the skills to make this more effective.

Given her concern with tracking children's schemas, Jennie was interested in finding out whether the children pursued these at home. However, she felt that there was insufficient time to talk to parents at this detailed level. In order to communicate to parents what the children were achieving in PDR time, she wanted to 'record more of what children are saying and doing in order to make sense of their schemas and persistent concerns'. She felt that she had insufficient help in the classroom, particularly as numbers rose during the summer term. She recognized that schools can either stifle or nurture children's innate abilities, but hoped that she was doing the latter.

Theories into practice

Jennie clearly valued play in both her theories and practice and had a reflective, analytical approach. She was well-organized, and had implemented managerial structures to support the PDR system. Although she strongly supported freedom of choice, this was in the context of freedom to plan rather than to just run around and engage in activities which, in Jennie's view, were not 'educationally worthwhile'. She perceived the need to manage the degree of freedom allowed. By her own admission, she had problems with play based on 'super-hero' figures such as 'Batman'. This indicates that she distinguished between play 'as such' and play 'in school'.

Jennie made little distinction between play and work, and accorded them both equal status, but did distinguish between teacher-directed and child-initiated activities. In the three videotaped episodes, Jennie chose to focus on the PDR session. In the first episode, she wanted to follow three children in order to identify the schemas they were currently working on and to see whether she could make links with her other observations. She noticed that Neill, who had poor speech and communication, had been 'covering things and burying things' but she could not articulate the significance of these actions:

> What I'm interested in is how does it link to the learning? I think it must do, because if the child is doing it repeatedly it must somehow be linking. But I don't know yet . . . I'm looking for those repeated behaviours. I'm hoping they'll build up into a picture over time.

Jennie recognized that some of her interpretations were speculative:

> Is there some scientific learning going on there, for example? While he's covering things up, while he's burying things, is he somehow finding out about the materials and the way they behave? Is it laying some sort of foundations for that later on? I don't know.

This theme of striving to understand the children's actions continued as Neill played alongside Claire: 'It seems to me they've got different motivations, different needs, different ideas.' She felt that this activity was of 'good quality' because of the levels of concentration, motivation, experimentation and absorption and noted that Neill was getting better at staying on task. She felt that he might have been working on volume and capacity, and noted that she could develop this in teacher-directed time to introduce the relevant language and concepts. Jennie made frequent hypotheses about the children's behaviour, but was less focused on the content of their learning, partly because the children's dialogue was limited and not focused on the activity. This stimulated her to consider whether this was just 'automatic . . . or occupational' or 'just pleasurable because it's tactile' rather than really 'helping thinking'. She recognized that just because Neill was doing lots of emptying and filling need not mean he understood the concept of 'full'.

Jennie was able to discuss broad issues but 'found it a struggle in terms of what he's actually learning':

> I think it's lots of things. It's being able to concentrate . . . play alongside somebody . . . copy good behaviour. It seems satisfying to him emotionally . . . and that's got to have a good message about school generally. If you feel emotionally satisfied and happy and contented in the environment . . . that's always going to help you in learning, because it's a place you want to be.

She viewed the videotape again at home and then provided a list of her detailed interpretations of Neill's learning (Appendix D) which shows detailed reflection and analysis.

In the second episode, Jennie focused on role play in the home-corner. Her intentions were to stimulate the play on the theme of a party as part of a topic on birthdays. She needed to be more informed about this type of play in order to support it, and again wanted the children to explore their own ideas so that she could look for schemas. Jennie's intentions were not realized as the children returned to the recurrent theme of 'babies and dogs'. She had already noticed that the children had been 'very quickly reverting to this baby play' which 'ends up in a lot of wild play' and felt that this was something she needed to change.

This contradicted several of her theories that children choose what they need, that they should be in control of their own learning and that play is developmentally appropriate. It also contradicted the PDR-High/ Scope philosophy. Jennie was unhappy about this tension and felt that by trying to change the play she had imposed her control. However, she considered that this type of play was not promoting learning, co-operation, decision-making, engagement or attention. Her intentions underpinned the play, but the children's intentions took precedence. The dilemma for Jennie was whether to support the babies and dogs or the birthdays play in order to enrich the quality of their learning. She rationalized this on the grounds that

> in the real plan–do–review philosophy it seems that you have the environment and the children then select things from the environment and you support totally. But, from experience, it seems to me that it helps if you have a stimulus. Sometimes it comes from the children themselves naturally. . . . At other times the play doesn't seem very rich in a certain area and it needs some sort of input to re-stimulate the play.

She reconciled this dilemma through close observation of the videotape as the children had taken some elements of the birthdays theme into their babies and dogs theme, and were showing evidence of interpreting and acting out their roles quite well. Jennie decided to support the children's intentions by focusing more directly on what they planned to do in the role play area in order to see how she could enrich the play through adult interaction and stimulating resources. Subsequently she used review time to talk to the children about it and discussed with them how to improve the play.

The third episode of play had open-ended intentions to allow Jennie to follow the children through the PDR system and to look for schemas. She felt it was not always appropriate to have specific learning intentions as following children's schemas in the PDR system allowed her to value play and the children's self-initiated ideas. However, Jennie returned to the dilemma of her inexperience at 'identifying schemas, following them, and then what to do with them'. She gave some specific examples to show how her thinking was developing, as in Michael's measuring schema:

> We sent a fax to somebody last week and they sent a fax back, and we watched it coming through the machine, and it was very long, and there was quite a lot of excitement about that, and it hit the floor. That leads into an investigation of how long the fax is, and his immediate words were 'measure it'. So he's got this idea of measuring, whereas nobody else had that idea.

Jennie wanted to work towards a curriculum model in which her observations of the children's schemas informed her planning of both
child-initiated and teacher-directed activities. She wanted to 'go a bit
deeper . . . how these patterns of behaviour link with thought', but her
inexperience in this area was limiting her understanding at that time.

Change

Jennie provides insights into how an experienced teacher managed
changes in her theories and practice. In some ways, she was behaving
like a novice teacher, going back to the fundamentals of reorganizing
her practice in order to accommodate new theories and insights. However, unlike a novice teacher, she had the confidence, skills and strategies to take risks, try out different approaches and implement change.
She also had the skills of reflection, evaluation and analysis and was
aware that she was testing out these new theories through her practice.

These changes were not a direct result of her involvement in the
study, as they had been fermenting for some time. She had already
changed her view of how children learn, her role in that process, and
the value of play as a result of working with a newly qualified teacher,
reading the work of a variety of early childhood educationalists, notably Athey (1990), and through regular discussions on curriculum development with a group of early years teachers. This had led to changes
in the way in which she organized play in her classroom. Using the
High/Scope curriculum model had enabled Jennie to raise the status of
play in her classroom:

> In the past it used to be that when you've finished your work you
> can play. Now I've changed completely from that to having this
> time when play is valued, when they can make their own choices
> about play. I never offer it now as the end of a small-group time
> session. It always has its own status if you like and we try and
> remember to call it the children's work time.

Previously she described play as 'domestic play, art and craft play . . . junk
modelling play' but had changed this to specific areas for maths, science, literacy, technology and imaginative play. This facilitated her own
and the children's organization, whilst still allowing some flexibility
between the areas. It also allowed Jennie to structure the play, thus
making it 'as rich and as broad as possible' and allowing greater choice
and autonomy. This was based on her view that play creates many
different possibilities for learning, and that her role is to support and
enable that in practice. Play was no longer a holding task and was given
more status. However, it is interesting that Jennie referred specifically

to play as their work time in PDR in order to give it more status: 'I'm trying to think of it in terms of their work and I'm trying to call it their work with the children and I'm trying to say ... things like "you've done some very interesting science today" or "you've been a good mathematician today".' Increasingly she was blurring the distinctions between work and play and talking more specifically about children's learning in both contexts.

Jennie's reading and enquiry into her practice led to changes in her understanding and interpretation of children's learning. She had used Athey's work to look at her practice in a different light: 'This was new to me and it was an idea that I was excited by because it seemed to get at the very heart of learning.' However, she was a novice in trying to implement these theories and interpret children's schemas or persistent cognitive concerns. This was raising further questions about the theories and their implications for her practice: 'I'm finding it quite hard to identify them, and identify them across the whole class. Some children display them more. So that's hard. I'm thinking, am I being fair and equal to the rest of the class?'

Jennie felt that managing her role in the PDR system 'gives me the greatest professional challenge' and was aware that she was not 'completely satisfied with my practice'. In the PDR system the children were supposed to stay with the activities they had planned. But Jennie had observed them wandering between different activities and was unable to decide if this was productive or not. Again this was seen as a dilemma between supporting children's choices and imposing her own perceptions of what was educationally worthwhile. She outlined key areas for development:

> I want to get better at monitoring play in my classroom and involve parents more so that we can inform each other about the kinds of play their children are interested and involved in. I want to be able to manage play better when my class numbers increase in the summer term. I would say that providing for and improving play experiences in my classroom are the things I have reflected upon more than any other curriculum subject or child behaviour in the past year, such is its challenge for me as an early years teacher.

As part of this challenge she tried to make herself available to support children's learning and not to 'clamp down on children's ideas'. Initially she distinguished between direct teaching and supporting children through their play, but talking about her approaches made her realize that these were complementary approaches, the difference being in who initiated the activity – the teacher or the child.

Jennie's critical reflection on her own development as a teacher enabled her to identify the impetus for change:

> It's only because of getting interested in it and going on courses and talking to other teachers . . . I mean you're constantly changing and developing and trying to get your practice better. It's what keeps it alive for me, I think . . . I've always enjoyed going on courses and being willing to change and ready to learn.

This willingness to learn and engage in the processes of change enabled Jennie to view her practice as a persistent enquiry into how young children learn. She was also able to identify what had changed and why it was significant for her and the children:

> I feel I'm beginning to understand more about why it's important to allow children to play and what is actually happening and how it's good for learning. Rather than being recreational or emotionally satisfying, there is something deeper than that, something intellectual, and I feel I'm beginning to get a bit more at the heart of that. . . . I feel I'm beginning to see the links of what the children are doing when they're playing and when they're working with me. . . . They're coming together and they're both valuable.

Jennie's data reveal that she was searching for new meaning and understanding from her reading and interactions with other 'like-minded' early years teachers. At times, her passages of intellectual search indicated that she was behaving like a novice teacher in striving to reconcile new ideas and ideals with everyday classroom realities. She was beginning to look for schemas or patterns of learning in the children's behaviour, but at this stage was unsure about their significance and how to support these through worthwhile curriculum content. She was developing the idea that children engage in 'free-range thinking' but again was unable to define accurately what this meant or involved. Similarly she talked about 'developmentally appropriate practice' in terms of children meeting their individual needs through self-initiated activities. However, this approach also stresses the importance of the teacher's role in providing challenges to move children forward in their learning (Mallory and New, 1994).

Jennie was aware that she was in a transitional phase in terms of her theories and her practice and found this both challenging and exciting. In order to move forward she stated that 'I need to do more study, I need more experience of looking at this, I need more people to talk about it.' For Jennie, her involvement in the study was 'the best thing I have done in years'. Her interactions with the research team had pushed her thinking even further, particularly in the final meeting where the group had begun to explore social-constructivist theories of learning. Jennie felt that at the end of the study she was left 'hanging on a cliff edge'. The process of reflecting on action had taken her so far, but in order to make further leaps in both her theories and her practice, she needed the support of a 'more knowledgeable other' and theoretical input. Jennie provides a model of an experienced teacher coping with significant changes in her theories and practice based on a concern to improve the quality of teaching and learning.

EVE'S STORY

Eve taught in a large inner city school at the centre of a housing estate. She had reception-age children, with three termly intakes. Most had attended a local nursery school, or one of three local playgroups and relatively few children had no preschool experience. She was concerned with the transitions between settings and had strong links with the nursery school, used home visits to get to know the children before entry, and encouraged children to visit her class for story time once a week in the term previous to entry. Eve taught in collaboration with a colleague in a parallel reception class. The reception unit was large and well-resourced for a variety of play activities.

Eve's theories of play

Eve had a strong commitment to a play-based curriculum and, in her narrative account, quoted a broad definition of play: 'Play is what children want it to be. Therefore it manifests itself in a variety of forms including arts and crafts, games and solitary behaviour, reading, imitation and so on' (Wilkinson, 1978: 68). Eve believed that 'to very young children play is work and they work very hard at it'. She perceived a clear relationship between play and learning which was specified in broad terms: 'Play is essential for the intellectual growth and social adjustment of the child because of the central part which language plays in it, in the way of imitation, discussion, general verbalization and problem-solving.'

These statements reflect the ideological standpoint that play is natural and is *the* way in which young children learn. Like those of Jennie, Eve's views were substantiated by reference to theorists and educationists such as Piaget, Smilansky and Athey, but also by her own considerable experience of observing and teaching young children. She was able to articulate this synthesis of theory and experience and described how she had tested and modified her theories in practice.

She considered that play had special qualities which encouraged the children to be deeply engrossed and to 'lose themselves' in ways which were not possible in more formal activities. Because of this, it enabled her to learn about their attitudes and dispositions as learners and to understand any problems they might have. This was a central preoccupation which is discussed more fully in her approaches to assessment, but is also related to the notion of compensatory education for children who lead fractured or difficult lives at home. She considered that different types of play stimulate different areas of learning. For example, imaginative play provides 'the basis of abstract thought and hypothesis' and helps the child to 'adopt another person's point of view'. Adult extension of children's language in play was also seen as a significant learning process in play. However, in planning the curriculum, she did not specifically classify play 'as such':

> It's all learning. What is the difference really between writing a letter from Goldilocks to the Three Bears to say you're sorry for messing up their house, or dressing up in the home-corner? In a way that's all play, or it's all learning, or it's all the same.

One of Eve's overriding concerns was her interest in children as individuals. Influenced by her Froebelian training, she aimed to find out what each child knows and ensure that individual needs are met by 'building upon' their prior experiences. Play was seen as an important part of this process as the children revealed characteristics not usually seen in other contexts. This was illustrated in Eve's account of an episode of good quality play in which two girls played cooperatively together showing multi-referential use of props, imitation, interaction with an adult, concentration and absorption. Usually, both girls 'tended to try to lead others and could be quite domineering in group situations' but behaved differently in a play context.

Teacher role

Eve was aware of the many different roles she adopted in order to support children's learning in a variety of contexts. She distinguished between a formal, didactic approach which she saw as 'authoritarian', and a more collaborative role in play situations. The former was related to whole-class sessions such as telling a story, imparting information or wanting the class to be a 'whole cohesive group', for example, in PE. Eve talked about 'changing shape' between this teaching role and a more collaborative approach in play. Although she was not explicit about this, classroom observations revealed that her formal teaching tended to be table-based and often involved some kind of recording for assessment purposes. The play activities planned were also structured by Eve and often included specific learning intentions or expectations. So play was not entirely free, the children were limited in the amount of time they spent at each activity, and there was less planned adult involvement. In spite of these distinctions, Eve did not regard children's play as sacrosanct. She was happy with the concept of taking on a role to interact with children in their play for the purpose of extending their knowledge and language and felt that they responded well to these two different roles:

> They are very different, but they're all part of being a teacher and I think that's what teachers do. I think they're very chameleon-like in a way and you can change instantly from being in a play situation and then having to immediately be in a quite responsible role again.

In contrast, her didactic role involved her directing and controlling what children do, as there are certain things which, in her view, simply have to be taught.

Eve's interactions with the children were either shaped by predetermined intentions or were responsive to the situation on an ad hoc basis. She felt that observation and knowing the children guided 'when to go in and when not to':

> It's difficult. But I think you can tell that sometimes you feel as though you might be intruding if all the children are so incredibly engrossed in a situation play-wise. But maybe they're not and maybe they need a bit of guidance into having, well, better quality play really.

She used a variety of strategies to improve the quality of play including extending language, modelling, mediating, asking questions and focusing children's attention on specific aspects of a task. She clearly believed that there is something special, almost magical, about the way in which children 'lose themselves' and become totally engrossed in what they are doing. Eve was reluctant to participate on such occasions, which she described as 'doing the big teacher bit', 'going in with your size tens' and 'taking over' children's play. So, her collaborative role meant being 'sensitive' to those special moments, and recognizing when it was appropriate to intervene and 'extend the quality of the play'. Sometimes this meant helping children to stay with an activity, for quality play in her view required concentration and engrossment.

Eve did not distinguish between free play and directed play and felt that it was sometimes appropriate to 'go in and direct it for a while and come out again, but not take over'. But she did not plan for this to happen other than spontaneously and expected other adults in the room to adopt the same approach:

> they shouldn't really intrude and really, really take over the play. Because in lots of situations adults take over . . . the play and the children follow everything they do.

This was congruent with her theories about children's ownership of play and the assumption that all play is intrinsically valuable.

Assessment

Although Eve considered that play had a useful revelatory function, she did not do any formal assessments through play. One of her central concerns was that play revealed children's worries and problems because they were more relaxed and uninhibited than in a formal situation: 'it's been found that children who happen to have been quite deprived, when they have had a lot more play experiences have come on in leaps and bounds.' She quoted the work of Smilansky, Athey and Froebel to support these theories and stressed the importance of adult interaction and working with parents to achieve these improvements. This diagnostic approach seemed more relevant to play than formal assessment and there was some evidence of how this information fed back into the cycle of planning.

Eve's interest in individual children extended into their play, which she often interpreted in light of what she already knew about them. This knowledge enabled her to plan for group activities where she had clear expectations of how children were likely to behave and interact with each other. 'Knowing the child' is, therefore, a key theme in Eve's story as it permeated all the data and informed her interpretations of children's learning through play. This was generally expressed at a broad level and on an intuitive basis:

> Oh, you can obviously tell all sorts of different things about the child's emotional state. You can see how developed a child's play is as well, whether they have actually played a lot before, or whether they're not used to playing with other children. You can see if they are frightened of something. You can definitely tell things that have been going on at home maybe that are re-enacted through play. Certainly the way that dolls and teddies are smacked maybe, or not, is a good indication.

She was aware of more specific learning outcomes and processes embedded in play:

> You can sit and listen to wonderful language actually. Conversations that have been heard, snippets of stories, songs that children know, how far developed, how mature children are in their play. And all sorts of learning. How many cups of tea they're making and whether it's matching up with how many people there are there . . . the curriculum side of things as well.

Again the work of Athey (1990) influenced the ways in which Eve interpreted children's learning through play. She talked about stages and schemas and how she used her observations of children's activities to inform her curriculum planning. She was consciously aware of these formal theories and how they influenced her own theories and practice: 'it's good that you do have a basis, a basis of some theory anyway, why they're actually doing that.' Like Jennie, she seemed to have taken on some new theories at a certain level, but was unsure at this stage of their implications for practice.

General teaching orientation

Eve's overriding concern was that 'the reception class should be an extension of the nursery' as she regarded formal schooling as both inappropriate to the needs of young children and constraining to her as a teacher. She referred to 'nursery ideals' which are founded on the belief that children learn through play, and admitted that 'ideally I would like to carry on a sort of nursery set-up'. In line with Eve's commitment to 'getting to know the children' as thoroughly as possible and on a personal level, she described home-visiting as 'the most important thing that we do'. In her view, only by acquiring this knowledge could she ensure that the children's individual needs were met by 'building upon' their prior experiences. This enabled her to start from where the child is and to respect his/her individual stage of development and level of achievement.

The curriculum was planned to integrate play and teacher-directed activities through a topic approach. The home-corner was changed to reflect the current topic (for example a garden centre or hairdresser's) and there was a variety of other activities on offer including sand, water, bricks, dressing-up, small world and imaginative play. These were located in separate areas although Eve saw them all as relating to each other and the children could transfer resources and materials between areas.

The children were divided into groups and were rotated through different activities (work and play) during the course of the day. Eve had specific intentions for each of the activities which were linked to the subject areas of the National Curriculum:

> usually if it is something to do with a sorting activity, that would be specifically mathematical. There would be maybe a particular scientific concept that you want to be gained from the water play probably. If it was linking in maybe with the farm, then you want the children probably to have some sort of empathy with the farmer, a shopkeeper maybe for the home-corner play. So, possibly it is basically to concentrate the children's minds when they're actually there in those particular areas.

Eve saw this form of organization as promoting the children's independence so that they are able to 'go off and learn as much as they can on their own, but with adult intervention as well'. This strategy had two aims: 'that is really a basic thing you want the children to do, to become as independent as possible, so that they're not always crowded around you and can actually begin then to be in charge of their own learning.' As with other teachers in the study, play thus fulfilled a dual purpose. It was appropriate for children at this stage, but also enabled them to 'make initiatives and choices and direct their own work eventually'. Because Eve had strong links with the nursery school, she knew that this approach was building upon their previous experiences. It was also consistent with her view that the curriculum in the reception class should be more nursery-oriented.

Eve was clear about the reasons for intervening in children's play, for example

> when play is losing direction. Maybe, for whatever reason, the children aren't motivated enough. Then you go in, then you would give the children some guidance. You would step in if you're invited in . . . if it seemed appropriate.

She was equally clear about when not to intervene and 'take over' and saw opportunities for extending children's play through, for example, circle time and discussion after the play event, based on her observations and the children's feedback.

Constraints

Although Eve consciously attempted to realize her ideals in practice, she recognized that some aspects were unattainable for reasons beyond her control. This was related to her view that school is not the appropriate place to educate young children:

> I was down at the nursery yesterday and . . . we were talking about the different constraints . . . the difference between nursery and reception . . . the reason that children have to go to school at a certain age, why should they?

She expressed the view that the nursery curriculum in which 'play is central' is more appropriate than the National Curriculum for 4-year-olds. She felt there was a danger that the pressures of the National Curriculum would filter down into reception so that they would have a 'watered-down' curriculum. Eve stated that 'in reception you get squashed between the two'. A further practical consideration was that the nursery phase is free from the artificial constraints of school. By this she meant timetabling and pre-specified hall and break times which create unwarranted disruptions to the natural flow of a play-based curriculum. Eve identified the higher ratio of children to adults in the reception class as a critical factor in trying to maintain the quality of children's play experiences. Because of the context in which she worked, staffing was a major issue:

> We've got rooms which are very, very big, but we don't have as many people as we should have to actually staff them. So you find sometimes you'll be on your own and there are quite a lot of children that you're dealing with.

This was exacerbated during the summer term when the final intake of children pushed numbers from around 20 to over 30: 'I'm sure that probably the play experiences would be richer if there are more adults around.' She captured quite accurately the complexities of working with this age group and trying to balance teacher-directed activities with play:

> It's almost like the spinning plates scenario, where you're trying to get one thing going, then another thing, then another thing, and by the time you come back then it's all stopped and you've got to keep that going . . . your time is being split up all the time . . . you're being cut in lots of different pieces.

Despite these negative feelings, she remained convinced that play was the most appropriate way for young children to learn and she endeavoured to provide a mainly play-based curriculum alongside more formal teaching. This was an accommodation to the realities of her situation but also represented a mismatch between her theories and her practice.

Theories into practice

In spite of her commitment to a play-based curriculum, Eve made a clear distinction between play and her own teaching. She did not distinguish between free and directed play, even though the curriculum was organized in such a way as to structure the play activities available to the children and to direct sometimes how they were to play. The thematic content was the link between formal teaching activities and play.

Eve had a reflective approach to her teaching and made conscious decisions about her planning and the adult's role, based on her extensive knowledge and experience of teaching young children. In line with her theories about play and the needs of this age group, social and cooperative skills were stated as learning intentions for almost all the activities observed in Eve's classroom. She recognized that children 'find it difficult to cooperate at such a young age' but considered that they could learn these skills through play. This strong bias may be attributable, in part at least, to her particular context and the wider ethos of the school. As she explained: 'it's an emphasis throughout the school and it's all to do with positive self-esteem and children turn-taking and everybody's important.' So, Eve deliberately created play situations where particular children could interact productively with others.

Although Eve was preoccupied with children's social and emotional development, her intentions for play activities were flexible and referred (albeit to a lesser degree) to subject matter and cognitive skills. Although she always had a clear idea of what she wanted the children to achieve in their play, she also recognized that often they also had an agenda which might, at times, take priority. But because the opportunities for learning in play were so wide-ranging, she felt that children were bound to benefit in some way, whatever happened.

For example, these multiple intentions were embedded in a videotaped play activity in the water tray in which the children were expected to sort teddies and boats by colour, play cooperatively and talk imaginatively about the journeys the teddies took in their boats. This was seen as an enjoyable extension of colour matching which integrated the term's topics on 'teddies' and 'colour'. As was shown in Chapter 4, the children followed their own intentions by filling their wrist-bands with water and in simply enjoying the experience of pouring and squeezing. Eve interpreted this positively: 'At this point it becomes a completely different activity. They're looking at material to see how slippery it is and how much water they can get into the wrist-bands. So they've changed the play completely.' Even though her intentions were not fulfilled, Eve considered this to be worthwhile, even inevitable, given the age of the children, as it was what they 'needed' to do:

> What they're doing is fairly good. They really are concentrating on their own activity . . . and they're testing the wrist-bands to see how much water they can hold, they're looking at the sort of material and they're concentrating really well.

She thought it was 'amazing' that so much came out of one activity and that 'you can become quite blinkered' by concentrating on teachers' intentions rather than on what the children make of the activity.

Different interpretations arose from an episode of construction play in which the intentions were to foster cooperative skills and to follow a picture to make an object from Mobilo. The children had done this before but in this instance, Eve had not made her intentions explicit to the group. From the start, Peter 'went off on his own tangent' whilst Susie and Dean studied the pictures. Dean then became engrossed in the activity, whilst Susie was clearly struggling to follow the design and needed help:

> They're just ignoring Susie. She's asked them for help quite a few times and they've just ignored her. Their whole body language is

they're curled over, very intent on what they're doing, and she's gone away and is asking for help from . . . other children in other groups.

Eve considered that her intentions for cooperative play were not realized, but her second intention was, as two out of three children followed a picture to make a model.

This episode raised several concerns. First, Eve reflected on the gender issue – the two boys were more competent at this activity than Susie, which suggested that they might have had more experience. Second, Susie was usually competent and imaginative and Eve was genuinely surprised that she was unable to cope with this activity. She reflected that she might have misjudged children in some areas: 'I've had assumptions about children, maybe that I'm thinking they're more confident than they are in some cases, and other children who I thought weren't as confident are more confident than I thought they were.' Eve also considered that this was a snapshot of what normally went on in her classroom and, because she was not able to interact in children's play as much as she wished, she was inevitably missing the opportunity to interpret accurately any learning processes and outcomes.

Change

Through her involvement in the project, and particularly the detailed reflection on action, Eve realized that her theories about play were not being realized in practice. She was clear about the reasons for this:

> I feel there are too many children, there are all sorts of different constraints. Ideally I would like to carry on a sort of nursery set-up really, but with more adults, and also continue play in a way for play to run its course, but I find I can't do that because there are too many interruptions.

These interruptions curtailed play and therefore affected its quality. She held on to the belief that play was important and that 4-year-old children should be following an early years curriculum rather than the National Curriculum. She was not able to put these beliefs into practice which she said made her feel very guilty 'because what you want to do and what you can feasibly do – there is a big gap'. However, Eve's data reveal that there were other constraints in her practice. First, by her own admission, she was making assumptions about what was happening in children's play which were challenged by the videotaped episodes. Second, she was making assumptions about children's capabilities to take ownership of their own learning and cooperate successfully towards agreed ends. Thus the quality of play was constrained by the children's age and competence.

For Eve, the main area for change was in trying to make time and opportunities for more adult involvement. Although she was comfortable with the notion of sensitive involvement in play she was unable to achieve this on a regular basis because of the context in which she worked. Similarly, her assessments and diagnoses of children's learning through play were somewhat limited in spite of her beliefs about the revelatory function of play. Because of the lack of adult involvement, the play had 'a more shallow quality. You're sort of skimming the surface really, I think.' Like Gina, she problematized aspects of her practice as a precursor to change.

So a significant element of change for Eve was realizing that her beliefs about the intrinsic value of play were not realized in practice. In order to address these issues, she believed that she needed the freedom to implement a 'nursery style' curriculum with additional support and fewer constraints from the wider school context. At first this seemed to be an impossible task and Eve appeared to be frustrated and disempowered. However, following discussions with the group, she began to see possible ways forward and decided that she would like to try the PDR approach used by Jennie and others in the group. This gave her a different framework for curriculum planning and organization which she felt would help her to reconcile her theories and her practice more closely. The dilemmas arising from the perceived discontinuities between theory and practice were commonly shared amongst the whole group and became a central focus for discussion as the study progressed.

GINA'S STORY

At the beginning of the study, Gina had just completed a Postgraduate Certificate in Education course, specializing in early years education. She had been identified by her course tutor as a promising teacher with distinct views about how she hoped to teach. The course had included sessions on the role of play in early learning and development, and organizing and managing play. In her first teaching post, Gina had a reception class in an open-plan school with a classroom assistant. As a novice teacher, she demonstrated in her story a strong element of development and change as she moved from idealized views of play to more pragmatic approaches which integrated play more closely into the curriculum and allowed for a greater degree of teacher involvement.

Gina's theories of play

Gina's narrative accounts indicated that she saw play as having distinctive benefits and as being an integral part of classroom activities. However, she was realistic about the problems inherent in play:

I regard play as akin to exploration, experimentation, choice, self-determination, negotiation and renewed challenges. The difficulty as a teacher is not only planning quality play experiences but also in extrapolating what has been learnt and in extending the experience.

The links between play and learning were made explicit:

Play for a child (and for adults) is a great enabler – there are no rights and wrongs and, most importantly, no major failures. Focusing on the challenge and discovery within play can only enhance standards (the child's own standards).

For Gina, enjoyment determined the success of play as a learning medium, as children are able to learn more easily if they are relaxed and happy. She distinguished between the intrinsic value of play and formal, teacher-directed activities which had more specific learning outcomes. She saw the children as being more motivated in their play than in teacher-directed activities, more relaxed and confident, particularly quieter children who were likely to be 'much more open'. This was compared with teacher-directed activities where children 'seem to get tired more quickly when I'm spouting on in front of them' and 'their interest isn't sustained in the same way'. Another comparison was that children did not seem to be able to work without supervision when Gina set the task, whereas in play, they were able to work independently, organize themselves and their resources and negotiate with one another. She also distinguished between free play, which is 'what the children choose to do without me directing them', and directed play, which is more 'teacher-led', such as teaching children how to play games with specific intentions:

I feel quite strongly that learning should be enjoyable as well as challenging like chess and other adult mind games. The problem lies in the word itself which has belittling connotations – 'just playing' or 'only playing' with the implication that no 'real' learning is taking place and certainly nothing of value.

For Gina the open-ended, enjoyable nature of play is at once a strength and a weakness. In her view it promotes learning but this is difficult to justify to those who regard play as the opposite of work.

In the early stages of the study Gina expressed awareness of her lack of experience and of how this contributed to what she saw then as a mismatch between her ideals and the reality of her classroom. At this time, her overriding concern was that play was the right way for young children to learn. She talked about her 'grand ideas about freedom' and her vision for practice where children are engaged in 'independent, self-directed learning' and are essentially 'free' to pursue their own interests and ideas. Gina believed that learning is most valuable when children discover for themselves as they do in play: 'I feel that they learn more when they discover, and often in a free play activity they discover something.' This is congruent with one of the key elements of the shared discourse on play, that learning must come from the child if it is to have real meaning.

In terms of the kinds of learning that take place in play, Gina focused predominantly on the importance of social skills and language, with some references to subject knowledge, for example maths and science. But her understanding of the learning content of play was relatively undeveloped at this stage, and, in free play at least, she stated that 'I am not expecting an outcome. Just expecting them to be free.' Independence was linked to children's ownership and control of free play activities, and to children taking responsibility for sorting out some of their problems without continuous reference to the teacher:

> They make up their own rules, they're highly independent when they're playing freely. And if they're not, if they come to me while I'm reading with a child . . . I am able to say, 'Can you go and sort it out?' and they are able to do that. Whereas often if they have a writing activity, they seem to want a lot of direction from me, or they don't seem able to sort out their bickering, or their noise level gets to such a state that I have to go and intervene.

In common with other teachers, Gina thus found that play has a pragmatic, managerial function. Her ideals about freedom and choice seem to take precedence, which may be symptomatic of her inexperience as a teacher and her wider philosophy of life:

> Adults would do well to return to the values of play, to discard the acquired inhibitions of adolescence and society and to rediscover the often buried imagination within us all. Like children, we perhaps need to take play seriously, use it as another learning tool and of course participate where appropriate.

These ideals contrast with Gina's narrative account of a good episode of play which indicated a strong element of teacher interaction in structuring the role play in consultation with the children, and in direct input to 'fire' imaginative thinking and to foster social and cooperative skills. Although the children were free to develop their own ideas, the defining quality of this episode was the reciprocity between the teacher and the children:

> Giving children ownership was also very effective. Where I was stumped for ideas they would offer a variety which stimulated my own thinking as well as made them feel responsible for the role play area and want to look after it.

Teacher role

Gina initially distinguished between her roles in free and directed play and was clearer about her intentions in the latter, though with some reservations:

> When it's a directed play activity that I'm involved in, we've been doing toys at the moment and we've been looking at toys with wheels and how they move, whether they move independently or what a person needs to do, and then it's quite didactic . . . my role. I'm presenting them with ideas and sometimes trying to draw them out, but I would describe it as more didactic really, which I'm not very happy about.

Her role in directed play involved teaching specific skills or concepts, for example counting, ordering and adding on through a 'stepping stones' game. In contrast her role in free play was more problematic:

> I find that when they have what I call free play, or they call planning, I'm not there enough to observe them and I think if I could observe them, then I would probably use it to take that into some sort of directed activity.

Gina felt that there were interesting or valuable things going on in children's play which would enable her to learn more about childhood culture and the content of their learning. For example, learning more about their language would enable her to 'capitalize' on it, 'because once I've learnt what they understand and know I can take that a step further in perhaps language activities'. She gave several examples of how she intervened in children's play with clear intentions, often asking for feedback or taking photographs as a record of what the children had done or made. On occasions she 'actually got stuck in a bit more' but felt this was not always possible or desirable. On the one hand, she did not have enough time to intervene as often as she wished. On the other hand, knowing when to intervene was also a critical issue:

> sometimes in the role play area for instance, adult intervention just stumps them. Once you're in there you've ruined it. They don't carry on afterwards because you've come in. But . . . when they're actually inviting you to come and see or come and join in in some way, then you can.

So although she held firm beliefs about independence and freedom, her pedagogical knowledge seemed to be leading towards a different view of how play might be used in educational contexts:

I'm working towards setting up each area in a very stimulating way so that children will learn. In the writing area I would like to try to put more envelopes, perhaps forms, or all sorts of little books and things that will stimulate them.

Gina felt that play needed to be challenging. Sometimes the children were able to provide their own challenges, but she recognized the need to make suggestions for moving play on where they were choosing the same things repeatedly. Even at the outset of the project Gina was aware that, as a novice teacher, her ideals were not always consistent with what she could realistically achieve in practice. The dilemma about her role in children's play was a consistent theme which she addressed during the course of the study.

Assessment

Gina's approaches to assessment also demonstrated the tension between the ideal and the real situation, and her own endeavours to establish herself as an effective teacher. As a novice teacher, Gina was concerned about accountability. This involved gathering evidence which meant 'children putting things on paper', and although she clearly believed that quality learning was more likely to occur in a play setting, particularly for children of reception age, this did not produce satisfactory evidence. In the videotaped episodes, Gina revealed that she was able to interpret the children's behaviour in relation to the value of the play context:

Michael is very resourceful in this and he's less disruptive. I know that he's very bossy, let's say, but he is less disruptive. He's more on task . . . he's making something, he's setting it up and he's keeping with it. Whereas often, if I've given him some writing to do or something that's more didactic, he won't stay on task, he'll scribble something in two seconds and he's not as interested.

Gina was aware of the potential for learning through play, but felt that she could not demonstrate this adequately as she was unable to involve herself as much as she wished.

Despite the lack of time and other managerial factors, she believed that her involvement was important in terms of children's learning. In her ideal situation:

I think what I'd really like to do very idealistically is set up a writing area and a maths area and a science area, and let it be relatively free and see what they choose and go from there. And perhaps work in one area one day with the children and work in another on others.

Gina indicated that she would like to teach through play within a fairly free and flexible framework in order to provide opportunities for assessment and to demonstrate the value of play to parents and other colleagues. However, there were a number of constraints which militated against this ideal situation.

Constraints

At the time of the first interview, Gina recognized that she was unable to realize some of her beliefs given the difficulties she faced in simply organizing and managing the children. A second issue was that being a novice teacher also brought with it an increased sense of responsibility and, moreover, accountability to external bodies such as parents, colleagues and inspectors: 'I feel a different responsibility to the parents than I did when I was a student.' The need for accountability impacted more on her as a 'real teacher' than as a student, particularly the need to obtain evidence of children's learning and make formal assessments of their progress. In her view, these constraints militated against the use of play, although she was aware of strategies she might usefully adopt to assess children's learning through play.

One of the major difficulties facing Gina was that she was not able to observe and involve herself in play as much as she wanted. This was primarily a management problem: 'the problem I have at the moment with free play is actually observing it and being there, because I'm a newly qualified teacher I'm trying to balance everything.' Often, when the children were engaged in free play, Gina would hear readers, which she felt was 'such a shame'. Children would play quite happily, because they were independent, which allowed her the time to catch up with other things. But, while she recognized that play during these times functioned as a holding task which was a conscious managerial strategy, she was clearly dissatisfied as it did not accord with her ideals. She wanted more time to be involved in free play because she believed that it would help in her assessments of children and that it would support their learning: 'I have got to try to free myself from reading and other activities in order to be able to observe children's free play . . . [and] to take part when they want me to.'

Gina did not see the National Curriculum as a constraint and had a pragmatic approach: 'If there's a programme of study to follow, I think that you could use a play activity in order to present a topic or something.' Other constraints were of far greater concern:

the constraints are . . . time, responsibilities to parents who don't necessarily see play as important as such or understand it. There are other constraints like presentation, recording what they've done . . . Also my own limited experience at the moment. That's quite a constraint because I should be capitalizing on all the facilities there are . . . and I do feel that's a failing in me at the moment.

Gina was aware of the tension between her ideals and the constraints of classroom realities. She talked frequently in her interview about what she *ought* to be doing, but contrasted this with wider expectations. At this stage, she was striving to reconcile her ideals for a play-based approach with what she perceived as other pressures and expectations. She had clear ideas about the ideal curriculum she would like to implement which included making play 'constructive, interesting and valuable', but felt at that stage that she had insufficient expertise to translate her ideals into practice. By the end of the project she had made significant changes to her practice through trying out new ideas and approaches. She also modified some of her ideals about freedom, whilst maintaining a commitment to play.

General teaching orientation

In common with all the teachers, Gina's classroom was organised on a self-servicing basis with a variety of resources and materials accessible to the children. She was happy with the amount of space and the resources she had to support play. The curriculum was structured to include a variety of free and directed play as well as more formal, teacher-directed activities. Play took place mostly in the afternoons to allow Gina time to hear children read. She had tried to integrate it throughout the day, but found this was distracting for other children and saw this as an aspect of her organization that she would like to change.

In spite of Gina's 'grand ideas about freedom', her general teaching orientation revealed a strong element of structure and teacher involvement. This represented a mismatch between her theories and practice, but as Gina gained experience, she made pragmatic adaptations to the realities of classroom life, and was concerned to improve the quality of play. For example, in Gina's narrative account of a good episode of play, the theme of Jack and the Beanstalk was used to integrate play with learning experiences in the core and foundation subjects of the National Curriculum:

> The theme extended to other areas of the curriculum – to dance and movement, history, looking at old and new – the candles became a talking point for this. One child said, 'They didn't have "tricity" in those days.' It occured to me watching the children at play that there was great learning potential even in items that seem so trivial. The important aspect is making time for review and feedback, also allowing time for ideas to formulate and develop rather than rushing into something new.

She felt that using play to free time for hearing children read or focusing on teacher-directed activities was not an ideal situation:

I do feel uneasy about it, because I think I would like to spend more time watching them play and from learning what they achieve or what they've done during that time. I would like to be able to incorporate it into other things, more directed activities.

Gina was aware of how she would like to develop the quality of play through better managerial and organizational structures. This would entail making her own teaching less formal and in doing so introduce a higher degree of freedom and choice, encourage children to become more independent, and foster positive attitudes towards learning. She was striving to find a way to make all her learning activities more like play in order to harness the motivation, independence and enjoyment.

Theories into practice

In each example of play chosen to be videorecorded, Gina had a high profile which contrasted with her theories about freedom, independence and ownership. This appeared to be a mismatch between her theories and her practice, but Gina realized gradually that freedom and independence could only be achieved within a clear structure. This was consistent with her general teaching orientation of structuring play and making teacher-directed activities more playful in order to enhance learning. She was adjusting to the everyday realities of classroom management and the complexities of teaching young children.

The following example shows how Gina aimed to make teacher-directed activities more playful. She initiated a language game with a group of children to encourage descriptive language, conversational and questioning skills and thought processes. Not only did she have clear intentions about what she wanted them to learn, but she was also involved in helping children to play the game successfully, first through teaching it on a separate occasion and, second, by being directly involved. By modelling the game with the children, she hoped that they would learn how to play it, how to negotiate, then do it by themselves and develop it in other ways. Although this was teacher-directed play, there were imaginary elements and opportunities for negotiating the rules which Gina felt still defined it as play.

Watching the videotaped episodes also enabled Gina to talk specifically about the evidence of learning in the activity. She made summative and formative comments about the children's social and language skills and their thought processes:

I'm really pleased that one child there thought about what the animal began with and that it came from the 'C' table, and obviously that tells me that they're taking things in, things that I've done before, because we've looked at words beginning with 'C' so it tells me that they're retaining knowledge.

Gina also reflected on her role in the activity and indicated points when she was deciding whether to intervene and for what purposes. She saw her role as that of a facilitator, which involved managing the situation, modelling questioning and conversational skills, and prompting ideas.

In another example, Gina had changed the home-corner to a shop. Her intentions were that the children should learn how to cooperate, negotiate, take responsibility and improve their language skills. She had already observed some of the children's play and was dissatisfied with what was happening:

> I have watched them play in their shop before and they tend not to play buying and selling. They don't tend to communicate very well. They do burglaries or they have guard dogs, and they spend most of their time . . . away from the shop area and chasing robbers or something.

As the children's play was not developing in the ways she hoped, Gina decided to change the content. She did this by preceding their play with intensive inputs (for example, stories and group discussion), thereby providing a focus and some structure. The children were more involved in setting up the shop, making toys for sale and laying it out the way they wanted with the intention that 'the quality of their time in there might improve and they might change the emphasis of how they use that area'.

Initially the children put prices on the toys they had made, again directed by Gina, but she was less sure about how the play would develop once the children were given more freedom. In the event she was pleased with the ways in which the children cooperated and negotiated as they set up a production line to make, price and display the toys. She made individual assessments of the children's learning and development, their individual characteristics, and the ways in which they interacted in this context:

> Watching this, there's definitely one person leading them in this and that's Jodie. John and Marie are helping. They're not negotiating the prices or 'how much shall we charge for this?' I was hoping for that sort of language, but I'm not sure that they're familiar with that anyhow, so it's probably something I can't expect.

This practice of structuring children's play continued with Gina using stories as a stimulus and a frame for the role play, with discussion of roles and expectations, children being involved in making props and in organizing the play environment. The following term Gina explained the thinking behind it: '[the children] are more structured, I think . . . I'm a little bit happier with that because I have more of an idea of what they are doing and what they are learning.'

The reflection-on-action interviews indicate that Gina was already beginning to modify her theories and her practice based on her observations of children's role play in particular, and her concerns that in the 'cops and robbers' play, for example, they were not really learning. She considered that the main reason for this was the lack of adult input to the role play. The relationship of play to learning and her own role formed the central theme of change for Gina.

Change

The degree of development in Gina's thinking and practice in a relatively short period of time is substantial. Even as a novice teacher she was able to reflect critically on her practice and problematize key areas of discontinuity between her theories and her practice.

The data reveal her overriding concern with reconciling these tensions. Her ideals were primarily based on notions of freedom and choice and were underpinned by her belief that 'school is about enjoyment as much as anything else'. In practice, she was presented with a variety of managerial problems and external pressures. These were summarized in terms of the responsibilities of being a novice teacher in contrast to her experiences as a student: 'My ideals haven't changed, but the reality at the moment doesn't seem to correlate somehow, doesn't seem to work. The curriculum doesn't seem to allow it in the same way.' Gina was aware that she needed to change some aspects of her management and organization in order to implement her theories. However, in the initial stages of the study, she was unable clearly to articulate what needed changing and how. Her perceptions of these problems were clarified by viewing the videotaped episodes of play, engaging in a process of reflection on action, and finding the confidence to change aspects of her practice.

In the initial interview Gina was often unable to articulate precisely what were her learning intentions for play activities. She expressed the view that she ought to be able to clarify her approaches, but had not given this enough thought, being a novice teacher. The process of reflecting-on-action enabled Gina to be much more specific about these intentions, and the outcomes of children's play. She interpreted children's learning in terms of both processes and content, and individual dispositions. Her intuitive understanding and tacit theories were thus made more explicit through this process.

The key aspect of Gina's change was in her own role. Although she still believed in the value of play and, indeed, continued to argue that play is a much more appropriate way for children to learn than formal activities, she also recognized that children need structure or, as she stated several times, 'play needs some kind of framework'. This again confirms the distinction between play 'as such' and play in school. In contrasting the unstructured 'cops and robbers' play with her more interactionist role, Gina recognized that the children had retained some freedom,

> although I did initially set it up, but they're still negotiating and discovering for themselves. It's down to them but they've got a framework. And I think in school that's quite a good thing.

A further strength of this kind of structured play, which retained some choice and independence, was that it provided a foundation for later skills in more formal areas of, for example, writing. Gina extended the framework to encourage the children to draw and write their own 'story boards' which encouraged them to think about their roles and the structure and sequence of the play as well as providing meaningful contexts for literacy. This also acted as a record of their play and provided evidence of their literacy skills which she could present to parents and colleagues.

This level of interaction in children's play represented a major shift in Gina's theories and her practice: 'my free thinking is more structured . . . and I'm trying to be more organized.' She recognized that her reconceptualization of play was pragmatic but was also related to the quality of play and learning:

> I have rethought things, but it has been necessary because it was just too disorganized and I couldn't run my classroom like that . . . I'm really keen to give them a quality play area that will take them a step further than the guns and robbers, I'm not saying that there isn't a place for it. It might be a vent, or something. But as a teacher, I felt the need to intervene in that and help them to negotiate much more than they do when they're involved in that type of activity.

After providing frameworks for the children's play, she was pleased with the result, and felt that it contributed to the quality of their play and learning:

> I think the children are negotiating better than they were at the beginning when I was much more free thinking . . . I'm reassessing what my priorities are. I felt that reading was really important. I still feel it's important, but there are other things that are important. Play, as such, came secondary to that. But learning more about the age group, I know that they need more of this type of activity . . . within more of a structured framework than I was originally giving them.

As part of this structured framework Gina saw more opportunities for linking play with teacher-directed activities, for example extending children's first-hand experience by visiting a shop to develop their knowledge, which would then feed into their role play. She perceived direct links between authentic experiences and role play which would enrich the quality of learning through play.

One of the main reasons for Gina's change is '[coming] to terms with this age, this reception and early years' and in 'meeting the needs of children of this age'. Thus her increasing experience of teaching young children contributed to her professional development and the changes in her practice. In two terms of teaching, Gina had managed to acquire some of the organizational and management skills she believed she lacked when she started teaching, and had reconsidered some of her earlier ideals. These ideals embodied the tensions between work and play outlined in Chapter 3. On the one hand Gina wanted to make all activities more playful. On the other she saw the need to make play more focused and structured and to relate it more closely to learning intentions across the curriculum. By the end of the study, her approach appeared to be more integrated so that work and play were becoming more of a continuum, with Gina being more aware of the need to assess children's learning in both contexts. She felt less threatened by external pressures and more confident that her ideals and practice were becoming more closely aligned. While many of her beliefs about the nature and value of play remained intact, her initial idealism had been tempered by the realities confronting her as a novice in the first year of teaching.

SUMMARY

These case studies show that the three teachers held similar theories about the value of play, reflecting some elements of the shared discourse between all the teachers. In spite of this there are individual differences. In their practice, play is regarded as a valuable context for allowing children to follow their needs and interests, develop intrinsic motivation, independence and a sense of ownership. These were seen as determining factors in enhancing the quality of learning in reception classes. However, there were significant differences in how the curriculum was organized to include play, and in the ways each of the teachers subsequently changed.

The use of narrative, semi-structured interviews and stimulated reflection-on-action combined to reveal rich patterns and layers of understanding and meaning for each of the teachers. The degree to which they were able to articulate their theories varied, and for different reasons. For example, as a newly qualified teacher, Gina sometimes struggled to articulate her theories as she engaged in a continuous process of trying to make sense of these in relation to her practice. At the same time she was coming to terms with the realities of classroom life as a teacher rather than as a student, and all the responsibilities this entailed. Gina's life philosophy initially predominated over her practical and pedagogical theories. This is an interesting point, as the initial teacher education course she had followed emphasized the importance of relating play to the curriculum through structuring the learning environment and having clear intentions which allowed for both child-initiated and teacher-directed activities. Gina's strong personal views about freedom persisted over the course content, although she seemed to draw upon this more as her theories and her practice changed.

Eve drew on a clear theoretical underpinning for her work which derived from her initial and continuing professional development courses. She was able to articulate her theories, but had already perceived significant areas of mismatch based primarily on the constraints of schooling. Like Jennie, she was beginning to engage with new theories about play and children's learning. She had started to restructure her thinking first, and then moved towards changing her practice.

As an experienced and skilful teacher, Jennie had some difficulties articulating her new theories and approaches, and had not fully got to grips with the meaning and implications of Athey's work on schemas. Effectively she was behaving in the same way as a novice teacher, but with a greater store of knowledge and experience against which to test those new theories.

For all three teachers, the approaches adopted in this study proved challenging and stimulated reflective consideration. It is interesting to note that where they were unable clearly to articulate their theoretical understanding, they drew on examples or stories of individual children or aspects of their practice to embed their meanings. Thus they were able to portray accurately their real life complexities, dilemmas and constraints. By examining their theories and practice, their stories contained a high level of reflective consideration, which, as Fenstermacher (1994) argues, is a minimal form of warranting knowledge and practical action.

All three teachers experienced some areas of discontent about their practice. Some of this was directed towards the constraints which mediated their theories and practice and which were beyond their control. But each teacher expressed dissatisfaction with aspects of her practice which could be changed through a process of reconceptualization. For Jennie, this process was underway before the start of the project and had included embracing new theories and approaches to her practice. Her experience and confidence enabled her to problematize her practice, take risks, test out new theories through her practice and engage in a continuous cycle of reflection and discussion with other colleagues in school. In the final group interview, she was particularly eager for more theoretical input to support her process of change.

Through observation and critical reflection, Gina also identified aspects of her practice which needed changing, and again had the confidence to tackle this in her own ways and in her own time. Gradually she made the distinction between play as such and play in schools, and between children's need for freedom and their need for effective managerial and organizational frameworks. Gina tried to maintain enabling approaches to play and learning, but within clearly defined frameworks.

Eve's discontent was more fundamental in that she saw the nursery curriculum as being more appropriate for 4-year-olds, and was tightly constrained by school structures. She felt strongly that she did not want to be pulled towards a 'chalk and talk' curriculum, but had to justify what the children were learning through play to parents and other adults. The way in which she organized play was prescriptive, in that there were intentions or expectations for each activity and the children were rotated through a variety of activities chosen and set up by her.

For Eve, viewing the videotapes challenged many of her assumptions about play and her own intentions. She realized that teacher-prescribed play activities are often changed completely by the children. Even where she had clear intentions for an activity, the children became engrossed in developing and following through their own ideas. This showed her that children think in divergent ways and that it was not necessarily a good thing to be too prescribed. She also realized that she was making assumptions about the children's capabilities to play in the ways she anticipated, and to derive the intended benefits from play. As a result of talking to other members of the group, she intended to change her practice quite radically by following the High/Scope approach used by Jennie. From feeling constrained and disempowered by her teaching context, Eve saw possibilities for curriculum development which matched her theories about how children learn through play, but which would allow her to address some of the problems in her practice.

The discontinuities between theories and practice were confronted openly by the teachers and provided a valuable stimulus to change. The case studies indicate that reflective consideration became a powerful means of learning and development for these three teachers, indeed was a shared outcome for the whole group. Each of the teachers changed their theories or their practice or both, for different reasons and by different means. But all held a common concern for improving the quality of play, and of children's learning, in their classrooms.

CHAPTER 6

TEACHING THROUGH PLAY: RETROSPECT AND PROSPECT

The principal aims of the study were to provide a clear specification of teachers' theories of play, to ascertain the relationship between their theories and practice, and to examine the perceived impact of mediating factors on this relationship. Fulfilling these aims was seen as the first necessary step in improving the quality of play in classrooms. Each of these aims will be considered in the context of the hypothesized relationship of teacher thought and action presented in Chapter 2. The constraints and dilemmas arising from teachers' theories and their classroom practice will be examined before exploring the theoretical implications for developing classroom practice and teachers' professional development.

TEACHERS' THEORIES OF PLAY

We hypothesized in our conceptual model that teachers' theories are embedded in their practice and are made explicit through their general teaching orientation. This incorporates their pedagogical priorities, which include the provision of contexts for play. The extent to which teachers are able to fulfil their ideal teaching orientations through the activities they plan for children will depend on sets of mediating factors or constraints. These will either enable or constrain the intentions and expectations relating to play. Finally, although it was not our stated purpose, the utilization of stimulated recall techniques generated a process of reflection-on-action through which the teachers problematized, and then revised, key areas of their theories and practice.

What then is the nature of teachers' theories? Clark (1986) has argued that 'teachers' implicit theories tend to be eclectic aggregations of cause-effect propositions from many sources, rules of thumb, generalizations from personal experience, beliefs, biases and prejudices'. Our data confirm that teachers' theories of play are indeed eclectic, but that the similarities between them constitute a shared discourse. This discourse was represented on a concept map, the key areas of which reveal how their theories inform curriculum planning, the selection of activities, teaching approaches, and assessment of learning outcomes. These key areas encompassed a broad knowledge base which includes ideology, child development, pedagogy, curriculum content and classroom processes, and revealed the interconnectedness of knowledge and practice, as well as their relationship to teachers' wider philosophies of the purposes of education, and the nature of childhood.

The teachers' theories indicated a strong commitment to play as an integral part of the curriculum. Play was seen as contributing to 'quality learning' because it provided the ideal conditions in which to learn. These ideal conditions included a range of learning-related processes, such as intrinsic motivation, exploring, experimenting and investigating. Developing positive attitudes was seen as a determinant of the relationship between play and learning because play allows children to be independent, develop their self-esteem, make choices, and exercise control and ownership. The idea of ownership was a dominant theme in the majority of the teachers' accounts and was related to the development of positive behaviours, fun and enjoyment. Play provided relevant, meaningful experiences which allowed the children to exercise autonomy and take responsibility for their own learning. Play enabled children to identify and follow their needs and interests, which revealed insights into their behaviour, learning and development.

Central to their theories of play was a distinction between play and work. Through play, children automatically matched what they needed to do with what they chose to do. This was contrasted with teacher-directed activities which may not always achieve this accurate match, or engage their attention to the same extent. In order to harness this intrinsic motivation and engagement, all teachers tried to achieve a balance, and in some cases, a continuum, between play and work.

TEACHERS' THEORIES AND CLASSROOM PRACTICE

Although there is increasing research on teachers' knowledge, there is little on how teachers relate their knowledge to classroom action (Fenstermacher, 1994). Similarly, existing research on teacher thought and action provides few indications of how the contexts in which teachers work constrain, or enable, the planning and enactment of play activities.

In order to provide these an interpretive, cooperative approach was required which aimed for 'quality portraiture' derived from teachers' accounts and perspectives. The resultant data revealed rich patterns and layers of understanding, allowing a detailed picture to be presented of the relationship between thought and action.

The teachers' general teaching orientation revealed that play was one of their pedagogical priorities and was incorporated into their practice in different ways. This occurred through the processes of planning, classroom management and organization, assessment and evaluation. Varying forms of structure were provided for the different types of play observed. There was a predominant concern with free or role play, but even this was structured to a certain extent through the resources available, and through curriculum intentions which were linked to the on-going topic or theme. Incorporating play into the curriculum did not imply a *laissez-faire* approach, and the amount of curricular free choice was limited. However, the teachers attempted to balance their own intentions with those of the children, in line with the shared commitment to choice, ownership and independence.

Role play was used extensively to realize specific intentions for a number of curriculum areas, notably literacy, as well as broader intentions such as social and language development. The ways in which role play was structured marked out the distinction between play 'as such' and play 'in schools' (Guha, 1988). This reflected the teachers' concerns that in a school context, play should be educationally worthwhile and integral to their management of learning. Thus role play could not be a wholly free activity, because the children's behaviour was sometimes disruptive and they did not always play in ways which were intended or considered to be educationally worthwhile. Typical approaches to managing role play included selecting groups to enable peer group tutoring, and to achieve a gender balance. All teachers structured children's choices, managed the degree of freedom and engaged in some social engineering to a far greater degree than their theories indicated.

Teachers' reflections on the videotaped episodes of play provided a realistic picture of the nature and quality of play in practice. These episodes revealed that their intentions were not always realized in practice, and that often they made unrealistic assumptions about how the children would respond to different activities. There was both over- and underestimation of the children's competencies, and of the degree of challenge in different play contexts. Where intentions were realized, the activities often involved adult participation, or some discussion prior to the play, in which the teacher outlined her expectations and helped the children to articulate their ideas. The discontinuities which they perceived between their theories and their practice served to highlight the mediating factors in this relationship, and these are considered below.

CONSTRAINTS

The hypothesized relationship between teacher thought and action suggests that there are a variety of constraints which may mediate ideals and classroom realities. The teachers' articulation of these factors allowed a clear picture of the impact on their practice of wider school and policy issues. Some of the more powerful constraints concerned children and the teaching context. With regard to the former, many of the teachers' intentions were not realized because they had unrealistic expectations of 4-year-old children, some of whom had little experience in preschool settings. They were learning to learn, to become pupils, and learning to play in school contexts. Because of the structures and intentions shaping play in school settings, the experiences and activities were qualitatively different for the children.

Mediating factors in teaching contexts included the pressures of the National Curriculum, space, resources, the daily timetable, adult–child ratios, and the expectations of colleagues, parents and Ofsted. The discussion of these factors in Chapter 4 indicated that their impact was different according to each teacher's context. There was a clear indication that contexts do matter in teaching, and that they either enable or constrain play in practice.

The teachers all felt that they had to justify play by providing evidence of the children's learning. This was problematic because written forms of evidence are given a high priority, and play provides few opportunities for this. So assessing children's learning through play was a dilemma. Where teachers were attempting detailed interpretations of the meaning of play activities to young children, they were sometimes hesitant. This was evident in Jennie's case study as she tried to apply Athey's (1990) schema theory and to understand children's mental representations through play.

Striving to achieve a balance between work and play was an integral aspect of their general teaching orientation, based on the concern to harness children's intrinsic motivation. However, this approach was complex and demanding of teacher time and expertise. An overriding issue shared by all the teachers was the lack of ancillary help with young children. The low adult–child ratios militated against the quality of teaching and learning to which they aspired. This is of particular concern in light of the common agreement among all the teachers that in order to improve the quality of play for 4-year-olds, more adult involvement is essential.

Many of the constraints and mediating factors were outside the control of the teachers and accounted for some of the discontinuities between their theories and practice. In the process of reflecting-on-action, they were able to identify those factors which could be changed, particularly where they were making assumptions about children's competencies, or where their theories were a constraining influence.

CHANGING THEORIES AND PRACTICE

Changes in teachers' theories and practice was an unintended, but valuable, outcome of the study and gave some indications of the processes through which this was achieved. Richardson *et al.* (1991) argue that genuine changes can only come about when teachers think differently about what is going on in their classrooms, and are provided with practices which match their different ways of thinking. Genuine change for these teachers came about through reflecting on their action via the stimulated recall of videotaped episodes of play, which raised their theories and practice to a conscious level of awareness. For most of the teachers this was the first opportunity they had had of observing in a detached manner the extent to which their intentions were achieved in practice. They came to recognize congruence and discontinuities between intentions and outcomes which led them to problematize, or think differently about, their practice. Cobb *et al.* (1990) similarly argue that the perception of practice as problematic is a prerequisite mental state for change, and that this comes about through reflection-on-action.

But simply reflecting on one's own practice is limiting. There comes a time when additional knowledge or alternative frameworks within which to think and reflect become necessary. For example, several teachers stated that, having watched the videotaped episodes, they needed to consider alternative theoretical frameworks for play, which included a rationale for adult participation and for extending children's learning. They were already considering changes in their role in play, but lacked knowledge of alternative theoretical and practical strategies to help them support and extend this. The teachers were able to draw on new knowledge and insights acquired through interaction and collaboration with their peers and the research team in order to restructure their theories and action. However, this was a unique experience and not one easily replicated more widely. Consequently, ways need to be found in current or new forms of professional development for the provision of new areas of knowledge and the provision of alternative frameworks if there is to be a serious expectation of change.

One of the major outcomes of the process of reflection for these teachers was the elaboration of a set of dilemmas about their practice. This set also constituted a shared discourse, since many were common to the group. Therefore it is likely that they may be similar to those experienced by many reception class teachers. These are thus considered in some detail below.

DILEMMAS

The dilemmas relate to several of the key elements of teachers' theories, and include choice and ownership, independence, discovery learning, the teacher's role, intentions, and assessment.

Choice and ownership

Play was considered to be a valuable medium for learning because it was based on children's needs and interests, and promoted control and ownership. Therefore the children did not require the support of an adult. In some cases, play was seen as a more valuable context for learning than teacher-directed activities because children automatically chose to do what they needed to do, and therefore exercised autonomy. Not only were these key elements of the teachers' theories, but they are also reflected in the literature on early childhood education.

Bruce (1991) affirms the ideological commitment to choice and ownership through free-flow play because it allows children to control and master what they have learnt to a greater extent than in any of the other processes of learning and development. Mastery of content, in her view, emphasizes that children have a sense of ownership about the content they learn. However, this standpoint was not borne out consistently in practice. Our data show that the teachers placed a great deal of faith in the youngest learners in school to plan their learning through self-initiated activities, or learn from teacher-directed play activities without an adult present. They were assumed to have a range of complex skills such as making decisions, carrying out their plans, cooperating with peers, sharing resources, problem creating and problem solving. However, the children did not always have the requisite skills and competencies to benefit from some of the activities. In some cases, the activity broke down and the children lost interest. In other cases, the children played to their own agendas and followed their own intentions. Some of the activities were virtually content-free, as the children were engaged in a hands-on capacity, but were just chatting generally with little 'brains-on' engagement.

The idea that play allows children to be free and natural is also challenged by the data. Free choice in each of the classrooms was not a real option as all the teachers structured the range and type of play activities on offer as part of their management of learning. These activities were underpinned by a range of intentions, to the extent that, on reflection, some were recognized as work-like (teacher-directed), rather than play (child-initiated). Even where the children did make their own choices from within these frameworks, they could not always play according to their own agendas, even where they were following their needs and interests. Some forms of play were seen as unacceptable if the children were noisy or disruptive. Thus the view that what children need to do is what they choose was also challenged in this study since the play environments were structured according to managerial and pedagogical considerations as well as to a range of mediating constraints. Without a high degree of consensus and control, play itself is of little value to the children and ends up being disruptive. Thus in order to allow some degree of freedom of choice, different forms of control have to be imposed.

Independence

The significance of encouraging children to become independent learners is linked to choice and ownership. The teachers had a dual perspective on encouraging independence. It was used as a managerial strategy to free them to attend to formal work, and was also seen as an important life-skill. The data challenge the view that all 4-year-old children are capable of functioning in the ways assumed by the teachers. The dilemma is that children do not become independent without acquiring the requisite tools for thinking and learning, strategies for socializing and cooperating, and for self-management. These are complex skills which do not just emerge spontaneously under favourable conditions. And providing play experiences does not automatically lead to independence.

The emphasis on encouraging children to become independent learners requires scrutiny. In order to be pupils in an educational setting, children need to learn a repertoire of appropriate behaviours in their play as in other activities. It seems ironic that young children are given more choices at the outset of their schooling than at any other time, in spite of their relative lack of experience as learners. Children may be able to manage themselves, for example by selecting and using resources, but this does not imply that they are managing their own learning. Therefore, children need clear frameworks within which to exercise their choice, and to be taught the necessary skills and strategies for carrying out and reviewing their activities and experiences. This involves greater emphasis on interdependence to enable the children to learn to socialize, cooperate and engage in peer group teaching. These were some of the intentions which were not realized in practice, again because of the age and experience of the children.

Discovery learning

It was widely assumed that because the children were exploring and discovering they were automatically learning. However, again this was not always evident in practice as the children's activities were not always followed up by the teachers to help them make sense of what they had explored or discovered. The primacy of discovery methods for young, inexperienced learners needs to be questioned because, as Meadows (1993) asserts, such methods only take the learner so far. Young children especially need to make sense of their discoveries and connect new knowledge with existing knowledge in order to make cognitive advances. Seifert (1993) argues that teachers should be aware of the limitations in young children's abilities to use cognitive strategies, as these cannot be used widely, effectively or consciously.

The data imply that teachers need a better understanding of how young children learn and how that can be managed in a school setting. The model of learning presented by Norman (1978) involves the inter-related processes of accretion, restructuring, and tuning. Learning takes place through a variety of processes such as imitation, social interaction, modelling by a more experienced learner, language, direct instruction and the input of new knowledge. Learning is a deliberate process, and children need to be consciously aware of what they are doing, learning and understanding in order to make cognitive advances. Again, evidence suggests that the metacognitive strategies which can make learning more effective and efficient need to be taught alongside meaningful content (Wood, 1988; Meadows, 1993).

The teacher's role

We found that despite the teachers' stated reluctance to intervene for educational purposes in children's play, they frequently identified the need to do so during the videotaped episodes. The dilemma was how to intervene and what strategies to use in order to move beyond benign questioning or brief interjections to check behaviour.

In spite of strong commitments to play, the teachers implicitly undervalued their role and directed their attention to more formal activities. There are two reasons for this. First, there were firm beliefs about play, particularly role play, as the child's world, combined with a general reluctance to intervene unless invited to do so, or to resolve disputes. Most teachers supported the children's language and skills development as the need arose, but this was mainly on an opportunistic basis. Second, the demands of the wider curriculum meant that a large proportion of time was focused on teacher-directed activities, particularly literacy and numeracy. After watching the videotaped episodes, they considered that the practice of non-involvement affected the quality of children's learning, but the constraints of time, adult–child ratios and school structures militated against more involvement. So the dilemma was that although they wanted to be more involved in play, this was difficult without reconceptualizing their role and the curriculum.

It was clear from the teachers' accounts that they did not see a clear role for themselves in children's play. On the one hand they held strong beliefs about the privacy of play, and the child's right to ownership. On the other hand, they lacked both the confidence and the practical strategies for meaningful participation. It is significant that in all the cases where the teachers changed their theories or their practice, or both, the role of the teacher and other adults in the classroom was a central feature of this process. This reflected a major shift in their thinking as they realized that if play provides valuable contexts for learning, then it must provide valuable contexts for teaching, and that they could legitimately be part of that dynamic. Thus challenging their assumptions about play also made them challenge their practice, and one of the key areas for change was liberating more time for interaction. This involved a reordering of priorities, a recognition that more of the curriculum could be enacted through play, but with a greater degree of intentionality on their part. This intentionality did not imply more teacher control, but included strategies for supporting children's ideas and interests in a variety of ways. Significantly for the teachers, they also needed to let go of the guilt they expressed if they were not engaged in more formal activities.

These aspects of change were particularly significant in view of previous studies which have been critical of the lack of adult involvement (Sylva *et al.*, 1980: Meadows and Cashdan, 1988; Hutt *et al.*, 1989). There was a broad consensus in these studies on the need for educators to involve themselves directly in children's play. Leaving children free to stimulate themselves, to be creative and to learn at their own rate (Meadows and Cashdan, 1988) was shown to have limitations, partly because of the age and developmental level of 4-year-olds. Although young children are good at learning, they have a limited base of knowledge and experience on which to draw as they encounter novel situations or challenges. The videotaped episodes show that children did sometimes experience failure, frustration and de-motivation which could not be resolved without support.

Teachers' and children's intentions

In spite of a strong theoretical adherence to the primacy of children's ideas and interests, most teachers had their own intentions and expectations for play, although these were not always made explicit, and sometimes contradicted those of the children. In some cases the teachers were unclear about the extent to which they should intervene and shape the course of the play according to their own intentions, which created another dilemma.

Assumptions were made about the relationship between play and learning, and about the children's skills and competencies, particularly in the socio-affective domain. Hence the 'automatic match' between the child and the play activity was not always evident. In many examples, learning intentions were defined which the children had already achieved, and the play context was thus used for practice rather than extension or new learning. In some cases the learning intentions were so broad that they covered a range of behaviours, again which the children were encountering regularly but without extension and development.

The idea that in play children cannot fail, or that play has success built in needs some qualification. There were many examples of children achieving a high degree of success in their play, either by following their own or by responding to the teachers' intentions. However, in other instances they often lacked the requisite skills to benefit from the experiences provided. The observations indicated that children often needed support with basic skills such as fitting together constructional equipment, sticking and fastening materials, and resolving disputes. Thus purposeful interventions which are responsive to children's intentions can extend play beyond the repetitive and mundane and thus increase the chances of success.

In some cases the teachers were confronted with the dilemma that the children's intentions sometimes took precedence over their own. This was more evident in the classrooms where the children were rotated through play and work activities. Even in the PDR classrooms, the children's intentions could not always be permitted free rein, particularly where this involved play based on television and super-hero characters, or which resulted in disruption or much repetition.

The issue of repetition raised another dilemma. How does a teacher know when a child is repeating something as practice, mastery or consolidation? At what point do teachers intervene to move a child forward, suggest new combinations, or teach new skills? These are difficult questions to answer as they depend on the individual child and the teaching context. Thus the view that children's intentions are paramount in play is another tenet of the ideological tradition that needs to be re-examined in the light of this study. Whilst many valuable opportunities were provided in the curriculum for the children to follow their own intentions, these did not always result in discernible learning processes or outcomes.

Assessment

The teachers' theories reflect many of the ideological tenets derived from the early childhood tradition. As such, play is regarded as multi-functional, providing rich contexts for learning, revealing a child's inner needs, fears and anxieties and allowing teachers to assess 'all-round' development. It was seen as having a revelatory function, showing where children really are, including the outcomes of their home and preschool experiences. It was also considered that play could reveal things about the children which were not visible in other contexts.

Three main tools for assessment were identified – observation, interaction and review time – but each had different limitations. The lack of time for observation and interaction meant that the teachers had insufficient opportunities for assessing children's learning. They could not interpret consistently the meaning of children's self-initiated activities, nor could they track what children had done in the more structured play activities. It was difficult for them to assess whether their intentions had been realized, or to understand the children's intentions and meanings. Hence it was difficult to provide a feedback loop into the wider curriculum.

Review time was seen as a valuable means of feedback but this relied heavily on the children's abilities to remember and report accurately what they had done, learnt or made. Here was another example of how a great deal of faith was placed in the youngest learners in school. Review time should assist teachers in following through children's ideas and experiences, and supporting these through further worthwhile curriculum content. This approach is an important element of the High/Scope curriculum model which had been adapted by several teachers in the study. However, as shown in Jennie's case study, this was a difficult model to implement. The success of review time depends on the children learning a repertoire of social and cognitive skills to engage in metacognitive reflection. As Wood (1988) and Meadows (1993) argue, young children have less reliable memories and need to learn strategies to assist memorization and recall. These cognitive skills need to be taught alongside meaningful content. That is, children need experiences which are worth remembering, from which they can make sense and construct meaning. More adult involvement in play was seen as desirable for assisting teachers' assessments of children's learning through play.

In summary, the dilemmas identified here were exposed and clarified as a consequence of classroom practice being problematized. The dilemmas shared by these teachers reflect the wider discourse which pervades early childhood education, and raise questions about the validity of the dominant ideology. The teachers' underlying theories embodied a mainly Piagetian, constructivist orientation which emphasizes the child actively constructing knowledge from interactions with the environment, resources and peers. This child-centred standpoint reflects the natural disposition of the child as an active learner, keen to make sense of the world through discovery and exploration. Childhood is valued in its own right, with unique stages which define the progression in children's learning. However, there is less emphasis on imparting a fixed body of knowledge:

children's educational development is not to be understood in terms of things that should be known, rules that must be followed, or adult characteristics that ought to be adopted.

(Darling, 1994: 3)

Piaget's theories imply that children cannot easily learn new skills or knowledge which are incompatible with their existing experience and understanding. Therefore a 'watching and waiting approach' is necessary to identify the next stage of development, with its qualitatively different approaches to learning. With the emphasis on self-initiated activity and experience, knowledge has almost been seen as a contaminant of childhood innocence. Bruce (1987) argues that learning is not compartmentalized – everything links, but with little specification of what these links are and how they are made. Similarly Nutbrown (1994) states that the early childhood curriculum integrates particular sets of ideas into a sensible and coherent whole. These standpoints raise critical questions about how and what children are learning, and whether links are made spontaneously or intentionally. Thus the processes of learning are emphasized, but appropriate curriculum content is not adequately addressed.

Piaget's theories have been interpreted to imply a reactive role for the educator, since intentional teaching and direct instruction were seen as having temporary and limited effects unless a need had been identified by the child (Meadows, 1993). The teacher's role in the current literature continues to be characterized as that of enabler and facilitator, with any interventions being sensitive and supportive to the child's intentions (Hurst, 1991; Bruce, 1991). Wood and Attfield (1996) challenge this standpoint and argue that such general terms do not describe adequately the complexity of the teacher's role, nor their pedagogical expertise. In their view a more proactive role in children's play is desirable in educational settings. Unfortunately this idea of teaching through play seems to contradict some of the central tenets of the ideological tradition, perhaps because it is taken to imply too much teacher direction or control.

Our basic argument is that many of the teachers' dilemmas arose from the predominantly Piagetian, child-centred orientation of their theories and practice. They were concerned to enhance the quality of learning through play by harnessing intrinsic motivation, creating opportunities for choice and independence, and by trying to make the curriculum responsive to the children's needs and interests. But it became evident that the quality of play and learning was inhibited by a range of mediating factors, most notably the limitations of their role in supporting young children. Although play seemed to provide contexts which were intrinsically meaningful and engaging for children, the conditions for learning were not always present. However, by the end of the study the teachers were beginning to consider how some of these dilemmas might be overcome.

Two key questions arise from these dilemmas. First, what alternative theoretical perspectives might help underpin teachers' attempts to improve the quality of play? Second, what implications for practice can we draw from this study?

SOCIAL-CONSTRUCTIVIST PERSPECTIVES ON TEACHING AND LEARNING

Meadows (1993) argues that in order for educational settings to become more effective, they need to adopt a Vygotskian model of teaching and learning. This is known as a social-constructivist model, in which children actively construct their knowledge, but with greater emphasis on social interaction, communication, and interdependence in the development of thinking and learning.

For Vygotsky, teaching and learning take place in the transition between two levels of development. The actual level of development is what the child can do without assistance. The potential level of development is what the child can achieve with the assistance of a more knowledgeable other who can be either a peer or an adult. The transition between these two levels is known as the zone of proximal development (ZPD). In the teaching and learning process, a child's performance can be assisted by interaction with a 'more knowledgeable other' who takes responsibility for keeping the interaction within the learner's ZPD, and uses language and a variety of non-verbal teaching strategies to facilitate the child's learning (Meadows, 1993). These strategies need to be responsive to where the child is, but should also promote further learning and development. In the ZPD, children acquire knowledge, skills, sense-making capacities and tools for thinking and learning, so the teaching – learning relationship is reciprocal rather than didactic.

How does this apply to children's play? Vygotsky (1978) argued that play creates zones for proximal development, because it is self-initiated and allows children to behave differently from the way they would in non-play situations. Play for Vygotsky was distinguished by imaginative action in imaginary situations, realizing intentions, using intrinsic motivation, the formation of 'real-life plans' and rules, and the exercise of will. All these features make play the highest level of preschool development in which 'a child always behaves beyond his average age and above his daily behaviour' (Vygotsky, 1978). An example of this is where children incorporate literacy-related activities and behaviours into their play, acting as readers and writers in imaginary contexts long before they have mastered these skills. Thus it is the social contexts of play which help to determine learning and development. The use of language is seen as particularly important as a means of communicating information, sharing meaning, defining roles, rules and relationships, and negotiating action.

In their interpretation of Vygotsky's theories, Newman and Holzman (1993) characterize learning as a revolutionary process in which new knowledge is not just acquired, it actually changes existing ways of thinking and understanding. However, this does not always occur automatically and the role of the teacher goes beyond that of enabler and facilitator. They suggest that because play creates zones for proximal development, learning occurs in relevant, meaningful contexts, and that teachers can create ZPDs through the kinds of play environments, resources and opportunities they provide. However, this does not imply a didactic, instrumental approach in which play is used only to fulfil the requirements of the legislated curriculum. It does imply a more proactive role for teachers in children's play.

Wood and Attfield (1996) outline a theoretical framework to justify a social-constructivist underpinning to the curriculum based on a balance between teachers' and children's intentions, and teacher-directed and child-initiated activities. This balance creates opportunities for teaching and learning through play, based on meaningful interactions in relevant contexts. The teacher's role is multi-faceted and includes stimulating language and conversational skills; helping children to create, recognize and solve problems; supporting cognitive challenge; modelling behaviour, skills and learning processes; and direct teaching of skills and knowledge, where appropriate. Thus children can acquire knowledge, make sense and construct meaning from their play so that it becomes educationally more powerful. Wood (1988) suggests that teaching children to become more aware of the processes involved in learning increases their abilities to use and transfer their knowledge and skills between different contexts. These metacognitive strategies include memorization, recall, reflection-on-action, evaluation, organizing information, communication, and forward planning, all of which can be taught during review or circle time. Children thus need to recognize the relationships between playing and learning in order to become successful players and learners.

In terms of curriculum content, the role of the teacher is to help children to recognize and make connections between areas of learning and experience. By these means they can transform children's needs and interests by connecting them with different ways of thinking and organizing information. The knowledge and skills which the children acquire through play form the building blocks of understanding which can be connected to the subject disciplines as an organizing framework. This involves beginning where the learner is, building on what they already know, and enabling them to learn new ways of knowing, reasoning and understanding. A social-constructivist approach implies a proactive role for all early childhood educators which goes beyond providing a stimulating environment, to considering how they might create the conditions for teaching and learning through play.

IMPLICATIONS FOR PRACTICE

Given the age and developmental level of reception class children, a social-constructivist approach seems to offer the potential for overcoming the teachers' dilemmas identified in this study. Although play was valued highly, its relationship to children's learning and development could not be taken for granted and many of the dynamic, learning-relevant cognitive processes were not always evident. This suggests that teachers need a more informed understanding of the processes of learning, the potential of a wide variety of play experiences, and the meaning of those experiences to children.

The teachers' theories indicate that play provides valuable contexts for learning, but that it was difficult to integrate play successfully into the curriculum and to capitalize on the potential benefits because of mediating factors. In our view, the missing dimension is creating the conditions for teaching through play. This is substantiated by the teachers' accounts and particularly their reconceptualization of their role in children's play. These accounts suggest that the following conditions are necessary for improving the quality of play in schools:

- Integrating play into the curriculum through clearly specified aims and intentions.
- Balancing children's and teachers' intentions.
- Creating a supportive framework for developing children's competencies as learners.
- Making time for quality interactions to enhance learning through play.
- Recognizing opportunities for teaching through play rather than relying on spontaneous learning.
- Freeing the teacher for more interaction in a mediational role.
- Teaching children the requisite skills and strategies for becoming independent, making choices and decisions.
- Providing a structure for review time so that children become more consciously aware of what they are doing, learning and achieving in their play.

In order to implement change, the teachers identified a need for both practical and theoretical support. Improving the quality of teaching and learning through play is not likely to occur without appropriate professional development at both pre- and in-service levels.

IMPLICATIONS FOR PROFESSIONAL DEVELOPMENT

The teachers in this study provide models of good practitioners across the novice–expert range who were able to articulate their professional knowledge and the relationship between their thinking and action. Their involvement gave them a rich source of data on which to reflect, enhanced their cognitive skills to engage in critical analysis, and the confidence to challenge their theories and practice. Their involvement also enabled them to raise their pedagogical knowledge to a conscious level of awareness which, as Fenstermacher argues, has important implications for professional development:

> The challenge for teacher knowledge research is not simply one of showing us that teachers think, believe or have opinions, but that they know. And, even more important, that they know they know.
> (1994: 51)

This level of knowing is particularly significant for early years practitioners who, as Anning (1991) argues, have been reluctant to articulate their professional knowledge. Athey (1990) suggests that this is because they lack a professional vocabulary that can clearly articulate the nature of excellence, but the reality may be that they lack the appropriate opportunities and conditions. When provided with such opportunities, the teachers in this study were able to articulate a rich store of professional knowledge, and to use this as the basis for reflection and development. They thus became 'change agents' (Manning and Payne, 1993) or proactive teachers who use informed awareness and deliberative thought processes. Proactive teaching is seen as an intellectual activity in which teachers use higher mental processes to determine what happens in classrooms. Manning and Payne (1993) outline a Vygotskian approach to professional development which enables teachers to use metacognitive strategies to guide their own thinking and action in order to become 'self-regulated learners'. This involves the processes of social interaction with knowledgeable others, scaffolding procedures, the acquisition and application of knowledge about teaching in general and one's own teaching in particular. Knowledgeable others can include peers and experts for, as Summers and Kruger (1994) argue, courses led by experts are better received by teachers and tend to produce better long-term gains in understanding. Thus Vygotskian theoretical perspectives are relevant for understanding teachers' professional development as well as children's learning.

This study has provided a rich conceptualization of teachers' theories and their practice in the context of play. It has also revealed valuable insights into ways in which the quality of teaching and learning through play in reception classes might be improved. Professional development is an important part of this process. There is a need for high quality teacher education courses which provide in-depth opportunities for reflection and evaluation to be more widely available, and at a range of levels across the novice – expert continuum. Short courses which focus on survival strategies and 'tips for teachers' are unlikely to stimulate the quality of thinking and reflection which are seen as necessary conditions for change and development.

Several alternative approaches to such courses exist, including action or practitioner research, and the direct teaching of new knowledge or alternative theoretical perspectives. What research in these areas, indeed research in the wider area of teacher change, attests to is the necessity of starting with the teachers' current practice, and enabling them, in whatever way, to problematize their practice through reflection and evaluation. Although these approaches are resource-hungry they are considerably more effective than most of what passes for professional development. They also enjoy the added advantage of giving teachers control over their own practice, and generating change through a practice–theory–practice model. As Fullan and Hargreaves argue,

> Teacher development must actively listen to and sponsor the teacher's voice; establish opportunities for teachers to confront the assumptions and beliefs underlying their practices; avoid faddism and blanket implementation of favoured new instructional strategies; and create a community of teachers who discuss and develop their purposes over time.
>
> (1992: 5)

The intentions underpinning these approaches are congruent with our own. We set out to empower teachers to fulfil their own intentions effectively through making their implicit theories explicit, and juxtaposing these to their classroom practice. Our aim was, and continues to be, the improvement of practice, and thus the next priority must be research on effective means of professional development. For, as Day (1992) argues, 'research into professional development is a contribution to a larger investment by government, school leaders, and teachers, in school effectiveness'.

TEACHER BIOGRAPHIES

Teacher 1 had 21 years experience, 18 of which were with reception-age children. She originally trained for the 5–12 age range and had undertaken two long award-bearing courses. She taught in an inner city primary school and had three intakes of children at the beginning of each term. (See Jennie's case study in Chapter 5.)

Teacher 2 had 15 years of experience as an early years specialist. She had taught nursery for five years and reception for five years. She had attended a Froebel nursery course whilst teaching in London, and had undertaken a Diploma in Education at Goldsmith's College. She taught in an inner city school and had three intakes of children at the beginning of each term. (See Eve's case study in Chapter 5.)

Teacher 3 had 15 years experience of teaching infants, eight of those with reception-age children. She was the early years coordinator in a rural school and taught a mixed-age class ranging from reception through to Year 2. Play was used as an integral part of the curriculum for all the children.

Teacher 4 had 12 years experience of teaching, with six years in reception class. She had originally trained for the junior/secondary age phase and was the deputy head of a large infants and nursery school. She had a mixed reception/Year 1 class with three intakes of children during the year, some of whom attended part-time. She had undertaken numerous in-service courses, and several long award-bearing courses.

Teacher 5 had six years experience of teaching, five with reception-age children. She had trained for the nursery/infant age range and taught in a rural school. She had a mixed nursery/reception class with three intakes during the year. The nursery children attended part-time for the first two terms, and the older children full-time.

Teacher 6 had just completed her first year of teaching at the beginning of the project. She had done a semi-specialist course in early years education during her Postgraduate Certificate in Education. She taught in the same school as Teacher 1 and had three intakes of children.

Teacher 7 had just completed her first year of teaching at the beginning of the project and had specialized in the early years age range during her Postgraduate Certificate in Education. She had a mixed reception/Year 1 class and taught in the same school as Teacher 3. She was undertaking an award-bearing course in technology.

Teacher 8 had just completed her first year of teaching and had specialized in the early years in her initial teacher education course. She had reception-age children with two intakes in September and January, starting part-time and working gradually up to full-time. She taught in an inner city infants school with a strong whole-school commitment to play.

Teacher 9 had just completed her Postgraduate Certificate in Education at the beginning of the study. She had specialized in the early years. Previously she had been a nurse, and had been attracted into teaching from her work with children and their families in hospital. She taught reception-age children in a rural primary school with three intakes during the year. (See Gina's case study in Chapter 5.)

INTERVIEW SCHEDULE

PLANNING

1 Can you tell me about the types of play you provide and why?

Probe: Explore distinctions between different types of play, and play and formal tasks. What differentiates these? Do these different types of play have different purposes? Do they relate to each other?

2 What, in your view, distinguishes play from other activities/tasks?

Probe: Explore benefits and special qualities of play. Explore play/ formal tasks and free/directed play.

3 How/what do you think children learn through play?

Probe: How can you tell? How do you know?

4 Can you expand on your understanding of learning and/or development?

ADULT INVOLVEMENT

5 Can you tell me about your role in play?

Probe: Is it different from your role in other activities and if so how? Can you make a statement about your roles in different activities?

6   Can you give some examples of when you might intervene in play?

   Probe: How do you know when to intervene? Explore beliefs about the nature of adult involvement and implications for free/directed play.

7   How do you assess play?

   Probe: Do you plan for this? If so, how?

8   What do you assess in play?

   Probe: Do these assessments feed back into planning and if so how?

9   How do you feed back to the children?

10   Have you ever come across the notion of scaffolding? If so, what do you understand by this?

KEY INFLUENCES ON THINKING AND PRACTICE

11   What are you pleased with in your approach to play? What is going well?

12   What constraints operate in the class, school, environment?

13   Can you identify any specific influences on your approach to play?

   Probe: What, if any, is the impact of the National Curriculum on your approach to play?

PRE – VIDEO QUESTIONNAIRE

Which play activity have you chosen?

What are your intentions for this play in terms of skills, knowledge, competencies?

Where has this intention come from? (i.e. does it link to previous activities, theme or topic or something else?)

How is the activity organized in terms of groups, resources and space?

Why have you chosen play?

Why this play in particular?

How do you think the children will respond?

How will you know if your intentions have been achieved?

APPENDIX C   CONCEPT MAP OF KEY IDEAS

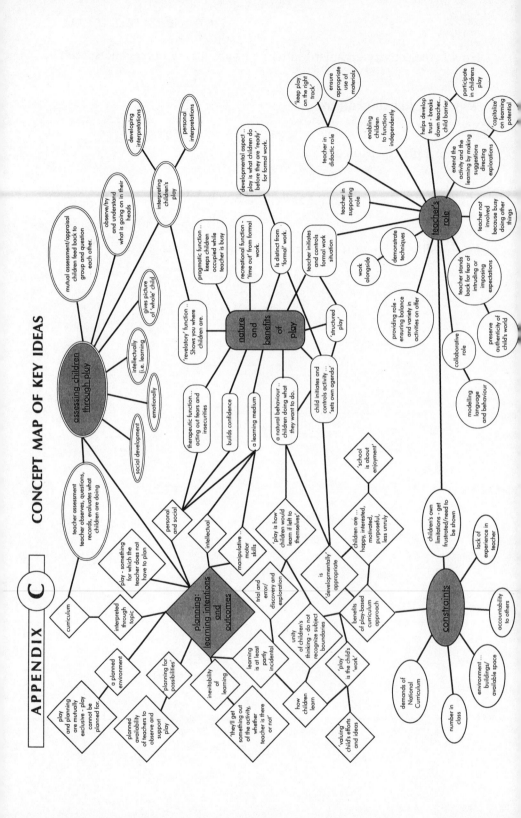

JENNIE'S INTERPRETATIONS OF LEARNING THROUGH PLAY

On first viewing a videotaped episode of play Jennie had some difficulty interpreting what a child (Neill) was doing in relation to what he was learning. Initially she tried to relate this to her understanding of Athey's work on schemas but felt she needed more time. A subsequent viewing of the episode produced the following detailed interpretation. This indicates that Jennie was striving to understand the 'deep intellectual processes' which are embedded in children's play. Neill had chosen to play in the sand, and was with two other children.

Pushing/pulling using the long rake. Experiencing forces?
He seems aware that the sand is sticking to things.
Interested in the qualities of the sand.
Making marks.
Pressing fingers into the sand.
Compressing it.
Levelling, patting.
Not encroaching on each other's space.
Cooperating.
Using a trowel to level the sand.
Making the sand into different shapes using his hands and moulds.
Getting ideas from each other.
Drawing lines on the flat surface, making marks (he is much more confident about doing this on paper now).
Shaking the sieve to make the sand loose.
Burying an object.
Filling a space again.
Compliant (Susie leading).
Selecting – this time a funnel for the 'ice-cream' cone.

Filling a space (funnel), levelling off sand.
Filling, levelling – a foot-shaped mould.
Estimating how much sand is needed to fill the small bucket; refills his
  spade with a smaller amount when he realizes it is too much.
Fitting 'bricks' together.
Controlling his behaviour in response to Susie's 'No!'
In review 'saying' with his hands what he was doing – levelling.

Jennie saw this approach as a valuable means of assisting her understanding of the links between external observable behaviour and internal cognitive processes. From analyzing what Neill was doing, she hoped
to be able to identify what he was learning, although she questions this
('Experiencing forces?') because there was no other evidence to help her
make an accurate assessment. Through this level of observation and
awareness, Jennie hoped to develop play activities which were carefully
matched to the children's schemas, what Athey (1990) describes as patterns of learning and ongoing cognitive concerns.

REFERENCES

Alexander, P. A. and Dochy, F. J. R. C. (1995) Conceptions of knowledge and beliefs: a comparison across varying cultural and educational communities. *American Educational Research Journal*, 32: 413–42.

Alexander, P. A., Schallert, D. L. and Hare, V. C. (1991) Coming to terms: how researchers in learning and literacy talk about knowledge. *Review of Educational Research*, 61: 315–43.

Alexander, R. J., Rose, J. and Woodhead, C. (1992) *Curriculum Organisation and Classroom Practice in Primary Schools*. London: HMSO.

Anning, A. (1988) Teachers' theories about children's learning, in J. Calderhead (ed.) *Teachers' Professional Learning*. Lewes: Falmer.

Anning, A. (1991) *The First Years at School*. Buckingham: Open University Press.

Atkin, J. (1991) Thinking about play, in N. Hall and L. Abbott, *Play in the Primary Curriculum*. London: Hodder and Stoughton.

Athey, C. (1990) *Extending Thought in Young Children*. London: Paul Chapman.

Bennett, N. (1992) *Managing Learning in the Primary School*. Stoke: Trentham Books.

Bennett, N. and Kell, J. (1989) *A Good Start? Four Year Olds in Infant Schools*. London: Blackwell.

Bennett, N., Wood, E. and Rogers, S. (1996) 'Teacher thought and action: teaching through play', mimeo. University of Exeter.

Berlak, A. and Berlak, B. (1981) *Dilemmas of Schooling*. London: Methuen.

Berliner, D. (1992) Telling the stories of educational psychology. *Educational Psychologist*, 27: 143–61.

Brown, S. and McIntyre, D. (1993) *Making Sense of Teaching*. Buckingham: Open University Press.

Bruce, T. (1987) *Early Childhood Education*. London: Hodder and Stoughton.

Bruce, T. (1991) *Time to Play in Early Childhood Education*. London: Hodder and Stoughton.

Bruner, J. (1985) Narrative and paradigmatic modes of thought, in E. Eisner (ed.) *Learning and Teaching the Ways of Knowing*, 84th yearbook of NSSE, pp. 97–115. Chicago: University of Chicago Press.

Bruner, J. (1986) *Actual Minds, Possible Worlds*. Cambridge, MA: Harvard University Press.

Bruner, J. (1987) Life as narrative. *Social Research*, 54: 11–32.

Bruner, J. (1991) The nature and uses of immaturity, in M. Woodhead, R. Carr and P. Light (eds) *Becoming a Person*. London: Routledge/OUP.

Calderhead, J. (1987) Developing a framework for the elicitation and analysis of teachers' verbal reports, *Oxford Review of Education*, 13: 183–9.

Calderhead, J. (1996) Teachers: beliefs and knowledge, chapter 20 in J. Calderhead, *Handbook of Educational Psychology* (forthcoming).

Carter, K. (1993) The place of story in the study of teaching and teacher education. *Educational Researcher*, 22: 5–12.

Clandinin, D. J. and Connelly, F. M. (1987) Teachers' personal knowledge: What counts as 'personal' in studies of the personal. *Journal of Curriculum Studies*, 19: 487–500.

Clark, C. M. (1986) Ten years of conceptual development in research on teacher thinking, in M. Ben Peretz, R. Bromme and R. Halkes (eds) *Advances of Research on Teacher Thinking*. Lisse, Netherlands: Swots and Zeitlinger.

Clark, C. M. and Peterson, P. L. (1986) Teachers' thought processes, in M. C. Wittrock (ed.) *Handbook of Research on Teaching*, pp. 255–96. New York: Macmillan.

Cleave, S. and Brown, S. (1991) *Early to School: Four Year Olds in Infant Classes*. Slough: NFER/Nelson.

Cobb, P., Wood, T. and Yackel, E. (1990) Classrooms as learning environments for teachers and researchers, in R. Davis, C. Maher and N. Noddings (eds) *Constructivist views on the teaching and learning of mathematics*, Journal for Research in Mathematics Education Monograph, pp. 125–46, Reston, VA: NCTM.

Connelly, F. M. and Clandinin, D. J. (1990) Stories of experience and narrative inquiry. *Educational Researcher*, 19: 2–14.

Cortazzi, M. (1993) *Narrative Analysis*. London: Falmer.

Darling, J. (1994) *Child-Centred Education and its Critics*. London: Paul Chapman.

Day, C. (1992) The importance of learning biography in supporting teacher development and empirical study, in M. Fullan and A. Hargreaves (eds) *Teacher Development and Educational Change*. London: Falmer.

DES (1989) *Aspects of Primary Education: The Education of Children Under Five*. London: HMSO.

DES (1990) *Starting With Quality: Report of the Committee of Inquiry into the Quality of Educational Experiences Offered to 3- and 4-Year-Olds* (Rumbold Report). London: HMSO.

DfE (1995) *Key Stages 1 and 2 of the National Curriculum*. London: HMSO.

Drummond, M. J. (1989) Early years education: contemporary challenges, in C. Desforges (ed.) *Early Childhood Education*, Monograph Series No. 4. Edinburgh: Scottish Academic Press.

Elbaz, F. (1990) Knowledge and discourse: the evolution of research on teacher thinking, in C. Day, M. Pope and P. Denicolo (eds) *Insight into Teachers' Thinking and Practice*, pp. 15–42. Basingstoke: Falmer.

Erickson, F. (1986) Qualitative methods in research on teaching, in M. C. Wittrock (ed.) *Handbook of Research on Teaching*, 3rd edn, pp. 119–61. New York: Macmillan.

Feiman-Nemser, S. and Floden, R. (1986) The cultures of teaching, in M. C. Wittrock (ed.) *Handbook of Research on Teaching*, 3rd edn, pp. 505–26. New York: Macmillan.

Fenstermacher, G. D. (1994) The knower and the known: the nature of knowledge in research on teaching, in L. Darling-Hammond (ed.) *Review of Research in Education*, 20: 3–56.

Freeman, D. (1991) To make the tacit explicit: teacher education, emerging discourse and conceptions of teaching. *Teaching and Teacher Education*, 7: 439–54.

Fromberg, D. (1987) Play, in P. Monighan-Nourot, B. Scales, J. Van Hoorn and M. Almy (eds) *Looking at Children's Play*. New York: Teacher's College Press.

Fullan, M. and Hargreaves, A. (1992) *Teacher Development and Educational Change*. London: Falmer.

Glaser, B. G. and Strauss, A. L. (1967) *The Discovery of Grounded Theory: Strategies for Qualitative Research*. Chicago: Aldine.

Grossman, P. and Stodolsky, S. (1994) Consideration of content and the circumstances of secondary school teaching, in L. Darling-Hammond (ed.) *Review of Research in Education*, 20: 179–222.

Grossman, P. L., Wilson, S. M. and Shulman, L. S. (1989) Teachers of substance: subject matter knowledge for teaching, in M. C. Reynolds (ed.) *Knowledge Base for Beginning Teachers*. New York: Pergamon.

Gudmundsdottir, S. (1991) Story maker, story teller: narrative structures in curriculum. *Journal of Curriculum Studies*, 23: 207–18.

Guha, M. (1988) Play in school, in G. Blenkin and A. V. Kelly (eds) *Early Childhood Education. A Developmental Curriculum*. London: Paul Chapman.

Hall, N. (1994) Play, literacy and the role of the teacher, in J. Moyles (ed.) *The Excellence of Play*. Buckingham: Open University Press.

Hall, N. and Abbott, L. (1991) *Play in the Primary Curriculum*. London: Hodder and Stoughton.

Hohmann, M., Banet, B. and Weikart, D. (1979) *Young Children in Action*. Ypsilanti, MI: High/Scope Press.

Holt-Reynolds, D. (1992) Personal history-based beliefs as relevant prior knowledge in course work, *American Education Research Journal*, 29: 325–49.

Hughes, F. P. (1991) *Children, Play and Development*. Needham Heights, MA: Allyn and Bacon.

Hurst, V. (1991) *Planning for Early Learning: Education in the Years Before Five*. London: Paul Chapman.

Hutt, S. J., Tyler, C., Hutt, C. and Christopherson, H. (1989) *Play, Exploration and Learning*. London: Routledge.

Isaacs, S. (1933) *Social Development in Young Children*. London: Routledge and Kegan Paul.

Johnson, J. E. (1990) The role of play in cognitive development, in E. Klugman and S. Smilansky (eds) *Children's Play and Learning: Perspectives and Policy Implications*. New York: Teacher's College Press.

Kagan, D. (1990) Ways of evaluating teacher cognition: inferences concerning the Goldilocks principle. *Review of Educational Research*, 60: 419–69.

King. R. (1978) *All Things Bright and Beautiful*. Wiley: Chichester.

Lally, M. (1989) *An Integrated Approach to the National Curriculum in the Early Years*. London: NCB.

Leinhardt, G. (1988) Situated knowledge and expertise in teaching, in J. Calderhead (ed.) *Teachers' Professional Learning*. London: Falmer.

Leinhardt, G. (1990) Capturing craft knowledge in teaching. *Educational Researcher*, 19: 18–25.

Mallory, B. L. and New, R. S. (1994) *Diversity and Developmentally Appropriate Practices*. New York: Teacher's College Press.

Manning, B. H. and Payne, D. P. (1993) A Vygotskian-based theory of teacher cognition: toward the acquisition of mental reflection and self-regulation. *Teaching and Teacher Education* 9(4): 361–71.

Marland, P. (1987) Response to Clandinin and Connelly. *Journal of Curriculum Studies*, 19: 503–5.

Maxwell, J. A. (1992) Understanding and Validity in Qualitative Research. *Harvard Educational Review*, 62: 279–300.

McAuley, H. and Jackson, P. (1992) *Educating Young Children: A Structural Approach*. London: David Fulton.

Meadows, S. (1993) *The Child As Thinker*. London: Routledge.

Meadows, S. and Cashdan, A. (1988) *Helping Children Learn: Contributions to a Cognitive Curriculum*. London: David Fulton.

Meckley, A. (1994a) Play, communication and cognition. *Communication and Cognition*, 27(3).

Meckley, A. (1994b) Disappearing pegs in the road: discovering meaning in young children's social play. Paper presented to the American Educational Research Association Conference, 6 April.

Miles, M. B. and Huberman, A. M. (1992) *Qualitative Data Analysis*, 2nd edn. California: Sage.

Moyles, J. (1989) *Just Playing? The Role and Status of Play in Early Childhood Education*. Milton Keynes: Open University Press.

Moyles, J. (ed.) (1994) *The Excellence of Play*. Buckingham: Open University Press.

Nespor, J. (1985) *The Role of Beliefs in the Practice of Teaching*. Final Report. Teacher Beliefs Study. Austin, TX: R. and D. Center for Teacher Education, University of Texas.

Nespor, J. (1987) The role of beliefs in the practice of teaching. *Journal of Curriculum Studies*, 19(4): 317–28.

Newman, F. and Holzman, L. (1993) *Lev Vygotsky: Revolutionary Scientist*. London: Routledge.

Norman, D. A. (1978) Notes towards a complex theory of learning, in A. M. Lesgold (ed.) *Cognitive Psychology and Instructions*. New York: Plenum.

Nutbrown, C. (1994) *Threads of Thinking: Young Children Learning and the Role of Early Education*. London: Paul Chapman.

Office for Standards in Education (OFSTED) (1993) *First Class: The Standards and Quality of Education in Reception Classes*. London: HMSO.

Pajares, M. F. (1992) Teachers' beliefs and educational research: cleaning up a messy construct. *Review of Educational Research*, fall, 62(3): 307–32.

Parry, M. and Archer, H. (1975) *Two to Five: A Handbook for Students and Teachers*. London: Macmillan.

Pellegrini, A. D. (1991) *Applied Child Study: A Developmental Approach*. Hillsdale, NJ: Lawrence Erlbaum.

Phillips, D. C. (1993) Telling it straight: issues in accessing narrative research. Quoted in Fenstermacher 1994.

Piaget, J. (1962) *Play, Dreams and Imitation*. New York: Norton.

Pope, M. (1993) Anticipating teacher thinking, in C. Day, J. Calderhead and P. Denicolo (eds) *Research on Teacher Thinking: Understanding Professional Development*. London: Falmer.

Raban-Bisby, B. (1995) The state of English in the state of England, in B. Raban-Bisby (ed.) *Developing Language and Literacy*. Stoke: Trentham Books.

Richardson, V., Anders, P., Tidwell, D. and Lloyd, C. (1991) The relationship between teachers' beliefs and practices in reading comprehension instruction. *American Educational Research Journal*, 28(3): 559–86.

Schoenfield, A. (1985) *Mathematical Problem Solving*. San Diego, CA: Academic.

Seifert, K. L. (1993) Cognitive development and early childhood education, in B. Spodek (ed.) *Handbook of Research on the Education of Young Children*. New York: Macmillan.

Sestini, E. (1987) The quality of learning experiences for four year olds in nursery and infant classes, in NFER/SCDC, *Four Year Olds in School Policy and Practice*. Slough: NFER/SCDC.

Shefatya, L. (1990) Socioeconomic status and ethnic differences in sociodramatic play: theoretical and practical implications, in E. Klugman and S. Smilansky (eds) *Children's Play and Learning Perspectives and Policy Implications*. New York: Teacher's College Press.

Smilansky, S. (1990) Sociodramatic play: its relevance to behaviour and achievement in school, in E. Klugman and S. Smilansky (eds) *Children's Play and Learning Perspectives and Policy Implications*. New York: Teacher's College Press.

Spodek, B. (1988) The implicit theories of early childhood teachers. *Early Child Development & Care*, 38: 13–32.

Stevenson, C. (1987) Young four year olds in nursery and infant classes: challenges and constraints, in NFER/SCDC, *Four Year Olds in School Policy and Practice*. Slough: NFER/SCDC.

Summers, M. and Kruger, C. (1994) A longitudinal study of a constructivist approach to improving primary school teachers' subject matter knowledge in science. *Teaching and Teacher Education*, 10(5).

Sylva, K., Roy, C. and Painter, M. (1980) *Childwatching at Playgroup and Nursery*. London: Grant McIntyre.

Thompson, A. G. (1992) Teachers' beliefs and conceptions: a synthesis of the research, in D. A. Grouws (ed.) *Handbook of Research on Mathematics Teaching and Learning*. New York: Macmillan.

Vygotsky, L. S. (1978) *Mind in Society*, translated and edited by Cole, M., John-Steiner, V., Scribner, S. and Souberman, E. Cambridge, MA: Harvard University Press.

Walsh, D. J., Tobin, J. J. and Graue, M. E. (1993) The interpretative voice: qualitative research in early childhood education, in B. Spodek (ed.) *Handbook of Research on the Education of Young Children*, pp. 464–76. New York: Macmillan.

Wilkinson, P. F. (ed.) (1978) *In Celebration of Play*. The International Playground Association.

Wood, D. (1988) *How Children Think and Learn*. Oxford: Blackwell.

Wood, E. A. and Attfield, J. (1996) *Play, Learning and the Early Childhood Curriculum*. London: Paul Chapman.

Yinger, R. J. (1986) Examining thought in action: a theoretical and methodological critique of research on interactive teaching. *Teaching and Teacher Education*, 2: 263–82.

INDEX

accountability, 50–1, 106, 107, 119
active learner, 80
adult-child interactions, 7–8
adult-child ratios, 51, 71, 99, 119
adult involvement, *see* teacher
    participation
adult role, *see* teacher's role
Alexander, P.A., 19
alternative frameworks, 120
Anning, A., 2, 11, 21, 131
Archer, H., 7
assessment
    case studies, 84–5, 96–7, 106–7
    dilemma, 35, 119, 125–8
    teachers' theories, 46–50
Athey, C., 81, 90, 91, 93, 96, 119,
    131
Attfield, J., 14, 127, 129

beliefs, teachers', 18–19
    and practice, 19–21
Bennett, N., 10, 19
Berlak, A., 72
Berlak, B., 72
Berliner, D., 24
Brown, S., 10
Bruce, T., 2, 3–4, 127
    choice and ownership, 121
    free-flow play, 5
Bruner, J., 12, 24, 25
building, *see* construction activities

Carter, K., 25
case studies, 79–115
    Eve, 93–102
    Gina, 102–13
    Jennie, 79–93, 140–1
Cashdan, A., 7–8, 13
categories, 28
changing theories and practice,
    76–8, 120
    case studies, 90–3, 101–2, 111–13
    practice-theory-practice model,
        132
    and teacher's role, 111–13, 124
child-centred ideology, 1–4
    and assessment, 126–8
child-initiated activities, 33, 87–90
children's ideas, 33, 39–40, 81–2,
    86, 115
children's intentions, 73, 88–9, 118,
    124–5
children's interests, 34–5, 45
children's needs, 34–5, 45, 62, 80–1,
    94
choices, children's, 34
    dilemma, 121–2
    structuring, 118
    theory/practice relationship, 60–3,
        75
circle time, 49–50, 126
    see also plan-do-review (PDR)
        system

Clandinin, D.J., 19
Clark, C.M., 18–19, 21, 24, 116–17
class size, 51, 71, 99
classroom contexts, 58
classroom practice
  beliefs and, 19–21
  changing, see changing theories
    and practice
  match of intentions with, 63–70
  match of theory with, see
    theory/practice relationship
  social-constructivist theory and,
    130
  teachers' theories and, 117–18
Cleave, S., 10
Cobb, P., 120
cognitive challenge, 7
cognitive development, 46
cognitive strategies, 123, 126, 129,
  131
cognitive structures, 11–12
collaborative role, 38–9, 94–5
colour matching, 69–70
'common law', 1–4
concept map, 28, 31, 117, 138–9
  assessment, 48
  constraints, 50
  control, ownership and teacher
    role, 36
  learning intentions and outcomes,
    44
  play and learning, 32
Connelly, F.M., 19
constant comparative technique, 28
constraints, 21–2, 23, 119–20
  case studies, 86–7, 98–9, 107–8
  teachers' theories, 50–1
  theory/practice relationship, 70–2
construction activities, 59, 66–7, 67,
  100–1
constructivist theories, 11–12
  and assessment, 126–8
context
  classroom contexts, 58
  play as, 4
  social-constructivism and learning,
    128–9
  teaching and constraints, 21–2

control, 80–1, 82
  teachers' theories, 33, 36–43
cooperation, 122
  match of intentions and practice,
    66–7, 68–9, 75
  case study, 99–100, 100–1
curriculum, 108, 115
  appropriateness of nursery
    curriculum, 98
  content, 20, 126–7, 129–30
  current perspectives, 15–17
  High/Scope, see High/Scope
    curriculum model
  National, see National Curriculum
  planning, 37–8, 43–6, 83
  teachers' theories about play in,
    43–6

Darling, J., 127
Day, C., 132
developmental level, 72
didactic role, 38–9, 94–5
dilemmas, 72–4, 120–8
  assessment, 35, 119, 125–8
  choice and ownership, 72–3, 121–2
  discovery learning, 122–3
  independence, 122
  management and organization,
    73–4
  teachers' and children's intentions,
    124–5
  teacher's role, 72–3, 123–4
discovery learning, 14–15, 104
  dilemma, 122–3
  teachers' theories, 39–40, 42, 43
disposition, play as, 4
Dochy, F.J.R.C., 19
Drummond, M.J., 4

Elbaz, F., 24–5
empowerment, teacher, 24–5
enjoyment, 53, 103
epistemic merit, 25–6
Erickson, F., 26
expectations, teacher, 119

fantasy play, 3, 5–6
feedback time, 49–50, 126

see also plan-do-review (PDR)
    system
Fenstermacher, G.D., 19, 25, 26,
    114, 131
free-flow play, 5
free play, 2, 43, 77–8, 118
Freud, S., 3
Froebel, F.W.A., 2, 96
Fromberg, D., 6
Fullan, M., 132

general teaching orientation, *see*
    teaching orientation, general
generalizability, 25–6
Glaser, B.G., 28
Grossman, P., 19–20, 22
group dynamics, 66–7, 71–2
grouping, 61–2, 118
Guha, M., 11

Hall, N., 13
Hargreaves, A., 132
Her Majesty's Inspectorate (HMI),
    13, 15
High/Scope curriculum model, 43,
    126
    assessment, 47, 49
    case studies, 79–80, 80–1, 90
    organization, 55
    see also plan-do-review (PDR)
        system
Holzman, L., 129
home-visiting, 97
Huberman, A.M., 28
Hutt, S.J., 8–9

ideas, children's, 33, 39–40, 81–2,
    86, 115
ideological tradition, 1–4
imaginative play, 59–60, 67–8, 69–70
independence, 74
    case studies, 81, 97–8, 104
    dilemma, 122
    teachers' theories, 33–4, 45, 55
intentions, children's, 73, 88–9, 118,
    124–5
intentions, teachers', 58–60, 118,
    124–5

into practice, 63–70
    match, 64–7
    mismatch, 67–70
interaction (assessment tool), 126
interests, children's, 34–5, 45
interpretation of learning, 46–50
    case studies, 87–90, 100–1,
        109–11, 140–1
interpretive research, 26
interviews, 28
    schedule, 135–7
intuition, 41, 47
Isaacs, S., 1, 2–3

Jackson, P., 1–2, 4
Johnson, J.E., 15

Kagan, D., 19, 24
Kell, J., 10
King, R., 9, 20, 23
kite-making, 65–6
Klein, M., 3
'knowing the child', 96, 97
knowledge, 18, 19, 117
    and classroom practice, 19–21
    imparting and curriculum content,
        126–7, 129–30
    need for additional, 120
    situated, 21–2
Kruger, C., 131

Lally, M., 13
language development, 45, 59–60, 109
learning
    constructivist approach, 126–7
    current perspectives on, 11–12
    discovery, *see* discovery learning
    Norman's model, 123
    social-constructivist perspective,
        128–30
    teacher's role, 14–15
    teachers' theories
        case studies, 80–2, 93–4, 103–4
        intentions and outcomes, 43–6
        interpretation of, *see*
            interpretation of learning
        play and learning, 32–6, 53–4,
            116–17

Leinhardt, G., 21, 25
levels of play, 7

McAuley, H., 1–2, 4
management, 73–4, 78, 108–9
Manning, B.H., 131
Marland, P., 19
Meadows, S., 123, 126, 128
    adult-child interactions, 7–8
    teacher's role, 13
Meckley, A., 5–6
mediating factors, see constraints
metacognitive strategies, 123, 126,
    129, 131
Miles, M.B., 28
mistrust of play, 11
model making, 67, 100–1
Montessori, M., 1, 2

narrative studies, 24–5, 27
National Curriculum, 35, 97
    constraint, 50, 70–1, 86, 98
needs, children's, 34–5, 45, 62,
    80–1, 94
Nespor, J., 20
Newman, F., 129
Norman, D.A., 123
nursery curriculum, 98
'nursery inheritance', 1–4
Nutbrown, C., 127

observable behaviour, play as, 4–5
observation, 38, 62, 107, 126
Ofsted (Office for Standards in
    Education), 10
organization, 73–4, 78, 85–6, 108–9
ownership, 74, 75
    case studies, 95, 104
    dilemma, 72–3, 121–2
    teachers' theories, 33, 36–43, 117

Pajares, M.F., 19
Parry, M., 6–7
participation, see teacher
    participation
Payne, D.P., 131
peer group teaching, 118, 122
Pellegrini, A.D., 4

personalities, 71–2
Peterson, P.L., 18–19, 21
Phillips, D.C., 25
Piaget, J., 4, 8, 93
    constructivist theories, 11–12,
        126–8
plan-do-review (PDR) system, 43,
    77–8
    case studies, 80–1, 83, 85–6, 87,
        89, 102
    see also High/Scope curriculum
    model
planning, curriculum, 37–8, 43–6, 83
play, 1–17, 76
    and children's choices, 60–3
    commitment to, 117
    current perspectives on
        curriculum, 15–17
    current perspectives on learning,
        11–12
    improving quality of, 130
    levels of, 7
    mistrust of, 11
    perspectives from research on, 4–6
    purposes, 55–6
    research on play in practice, 6–11
    teacher's role, 13–15
    teachers' theories, 32–6, 53–4,
        116–17
    traditions and ideologies, 2–4
    and work, see work
play tutoring, 5
Pope, M., 19
Post Office, 68–9
practical reasoning, 25, 76
practice, classroom, see classroom
    practice
practice-theory-practice model, 132
proactive teaching, 131
professional development, 130–2
provider, teacher as, 37–8
proximal development, zones of,
    (ZPDs), 12, 128–9

Raban-Bisby, B., 57
reflection, 24, 132
    changing theories and practice,
        76–8, 114–15, 120

repetition, 125
review time, 49–50, 126
    see also plan-do-review (PDR)
        system
Richardson, V., 20, 120
role play, 58, 118
    approaches to managing, 118
    case studies, 83, 88–9, 110–11
    Post Office, 68–9
    Snow White, 64–5
    teachers' intentions, 59, 59–60
        match with practice, 64–5,
            68–9, 75
    teacher's role, 40–3
Rumbold Report, 16

sand play, 59
schemas (patterns of learning), 81,
    87–90, 91, 92
Schoenfield, A., 21
secondary school teachers, 20
Seifert, K.L., 15, 123
self-regulated learners, 131
sensitive intervention, 39–40, 40–2,
    82, 125
Sestini, E., 9–10
Shefatya, L., 13–14
shop play, 110
situated knowledge, 21–2
small world play, 59
Smilansky, S., 5, 13, 14, 93, 96
social-constructivist theories, 12, 14
    perspectives on teaching and
        learning, 128–30
social development, 12, 45, 59–60,
    75, 99–100, 122
social interaction, 12, 45, 61–2, 69–70
socio-affective domain, 45
sociodramatic play, 3, 5–6
Spodek, B., 20–1
Steiner, R., 1, 2
Stevenson, C., 10
stimulated recall, 25–6
Stodolsky, S., 22
story-telling, 24–5, 27
Strauss, A.L., 28
structured play, 43, 74, 75, 118
    case studies, 109–10, 111–12

student teachers, 19–20
Summers, M., 131
support (sensitive intervention),
    39–40, 40–2, 82, 125
Sylva, K., 7

tasks, nature of, 58
teacher biographies, 133–4
teacher-directed activities, 87–90,
    103
    see also work
teacher group meetings, 27, 28,
    29–30
teacher participation, 38–40, 62
    case studies, 102, 104, 106, 107
    changing practice, 78
    constraints, 72, 75, 107
    dilemma, 123–4
    in role play, 40–3
teachers' intentions, see intentions,
    teachers'
teacher's role, 13–15, 75
    case studies, 82–4, 94–5, 105–6,
        111–13
    change, 111–13, 124
    child-centred ideology, 3, 127
    dilemma, 72–3, 123–4
    observer, 38
    participant, 38–40
    provider, 37–8
    research on play, 7–10
    role play, 40–3
    social-constructivist perspectives,
        14–15, 129–30
    teachers' theories, 36–43, 53
teachers' theories, 21, 31–56, 116–17
    assessment, 46–50
    case studies, 80–2, 93–4, 102–4,
        113–14
    and classroom practice, 117–18
    constraints, 50–1
    control, 33, 36–43
    general teaching orientation, 54–6
    learning intentions and outcomes,
        43–6
    ownership, 33, 36–43, 117
    play and learning, 32–6, 53–4,
        116–17

play and work, 51–4
teacher's role, 36–43, 53
see also theory/practice relationship
teaching orientation, general, 54–6,
    118
  case studies, 85–6, 97–8, 108–9
theory/practice relationship, 18–30,
    57–78
  case studies, 87–90, 99–101,
    109–11, 114–15
  change, 76–8, 114–15
  children's choices, 60–3, 75
  classroom contexts and nature of
    tasks, 58
  constraints, 70–2
  dilemmas, 72–4
  intentions and practice, 63–70
    match, 64–7
    mismatch, 67–70
  methodological considerations,
    24–6
  model, 22–4
  research design, 26–30
  teachers' intentions, 58–60

Thompson, A.G., 20
tutorial dialogue, 8

validity, 25–6, 30
videotape recordings, 28–30
Vygotsky, L., 12, 128–9, 131

Walsh, D.J., 26
warranting knowledge, 25–6, 30
water play, 67–8, 69–70, 100
Wilkinson, P.F., 93
Wood, D., 126, 129
Wood, E.A., 14, 127, 129
work
  assessment and, 35, 47
  play and, 51–4, 117
    continuum, 4–5, 55, 113
wrist-bands, 69–70
writing, 112

Yinger, R.J., 26

zones of proximal development
    (ZPDs), 12, 128–9

A NATIONAL CURRICULUM FOR THE EARLY YEARS

Angela Anning (ed.)

- What does the National Curriculum mean to pupils and teachers at Key Stage One?
- How have teachers and children coped with the ongoing changes?
- How has subject teaching altered in infant classrooms?

In *A National Curriculum for the Early Years*, Angela Anning and her team of contributors set out to examine these issues. Infant teachers and their pupils were the guinea pigs for the introduction of the National Curriculum over a five-year period. Despite many reservations about a subject-based curriculum for young children, teachers struggled to interpret the National Curriculum Orders into a workable, if not manageable, curriculum in their classrooms.

The contributors to this book, each experts in a subject discipline, have kept in close touch with practising and intending infant teachers as the National Curriculum was operationalized in primary schools. They have used their teacher networks, as well as research evidence, to tap into the strategies used by infant teachers to cope with the planning, delivery and assessment of the National Curriculum subjects and the effects of government policy changes on young children's learning.

Together the contributors provide a timely analysis of subject discipline based education for young children and look ahead to the prospects for those subjects at Key Stage One in the second half of the 1990s.

This book will be essential reading for anyone involved in the education of young children.

Contents
A National Curriculum for Key Stage One – English – Mathematics – Science – Design and Technology and Information Technology – Geography – History – Art – Music – Physical Education – Religious Education – The way ahead: Another National Curriculum for Key Stage One? – Author index – Subject index.

Contributors
Angela Anning, Hilary Asoko, Roger Beard, Eileen Bellett, Helen Constable, David Dawson, Carolyn Jones, Ann MacNamara, Elizabeth Wood, Patrick Wiegand.

176pp   0 335 19431 1 (Paperback)   0 335 19432 X (Hardback)

THE FIRST YEARS AT SCHOOL (Second Edition)
EDUCATION 4 TO 8

Angela Anning

Review of the First Edition:

"I found the whole account a model of clarity with a good blend of theory and practice which many authors would do well to note."

Ted Wragg, *Times Educational Supplement*

The First Years at School (Second Edition) is a practical and reflective discussion of the education of 4 to 8-year-olds based on a sympathetic recognition of the complexities of being an early years teacher. Angela Anning begins by reviewing the historical and ideological traditions of British infant and primary schools, tracing how we have reached the position where teachers are torn between child-centred progressivism and utilitarian demands in educating young children. She then provides a detailed and authoritative critique of recent thinking about the cognitive, social and emotional development of children; and explores the complexities of teachers' roles, particularly in the areas of language, intervention and expectations. She discusses the organization of the classroom, the structuring of learning in the school day and the content of the curriculum. She tackles the implications of the series of changes in the National Curriculum Orders and national assessment systems for 7-year-olds and their impact on pre-5s and children with special educational needs. The second edition brings the debate about the post-Dearing Key Stage 1 curriculum and its implications for pre-school education bang up-to-date. This will be vital reading for both student and practising teachers of young children.

Contents
Histories and ideologies – Children learning – Teachers teaching – The curriculum – A National Curriculum for 4 to 8-year-olds – Beyond the new ERA – References – Name index – Subject index.

184pp   0 335 19690 X (Paperback)